THE SEX BOOK

A MODERN PICTORIAL ENCYCLOPEDIA

Text: Martin Goldstein M.D.
and Erwin J. Haeberle Ph.D.
Photography: Will McBride

What is love?

Can a girl get pregnant during her period?

Is abortion murder?

WHY AM I A HOMOSEXUAL?

Do you have trouble maintaining an erection when playing a passive role?

Why is prostitution illegal?

What is a transvestite?

CAN Small Childeen MASTURBATE?

WHY ARE PEOPLE SO SECRET ABOUT THEIR SEXUAL EMOTIONS AND FEELINGS?

Can one find sexual fulfillment through one-night stands exclusively?

Can you have sex when you are pregnant?

Do two men make love the same way as two women?

In consummating the sex act is the withdrawal method physically harmful for the male?

Is there any advantage to being circumcized?

What is a nymphomaniac?

How long does intercourse normally last?

What can one do about premature ejaculation?

HOW SAFE ARE THE VARIOUS METHODS OF BIRTH-CONTROL.

CAN A FEMALE ATTAIN SEXUAL SATISFACTION WITHOUT EXPERIENCING AN ORGASM?

Do more males feel the need to masturbate than females.

How often can one masturbate?

WHEN DOES THE EMBRYO BECOME A FETUS?

What is a Sexual perversion?

What is the Electra Complex?

CAN A PERSON LOVE AND HATE ANOTHER PERSON AT THE SAME TIME?

What do you think about oral sex?

Do you feel that pre-marital sex is healthy before marriage or that it is harmful?

Do you ever have sexual nightmares?

At what age do people stop having sex?

Why don't people understand what love is?

This is a book for young people and their parents. It deals with sex in an honest and straightforward manner, and thus hopes to contribute to mutual understanding and trust not only between the sexes, but also between the generations. In the past, sex was often allowed to create fear, guilt, and despair when it should have inspired faith, hope and love. People frequently did not dare to inquire into everything they wanted to know about sex. Many adults today remember their own lonely search for answers, and now seek to give their children an adequate sex education. The present work can help them in this effort.

However, the importance of sex education goes beyond the private concerns of the individual family. This was recently emphasized by the Federal Commission on Obscenity and Pornography, whose official report "recommends that a massive sex education effort be launched. . . . It should be aimed at achieving an acceptance of sex as a normal and natural part of life and of oneself as a sexual being. It should not aim for orthodoxy; rather, it should be designed to allow for a pluralism of values. It should be based on facts and encompass not only biological and physiological information but also social, psychological and religious information. . . . It should be aimed, as appropriate, to all segments of our society, adults as well as children and adolescents."

THE SEX BOOK tries to follow the letter as well as the spirit of these recommendations.

Obviously, like any other book, it had to accept certain limitations. The authors could not, in a single volume, present a compendium of all the available biological, anthropological, medical, legal, sociological, and religious knowledge. Neither did they intend to offer a substitute for personal counselling. Their aim was to provide an esthetically pleasing book that would give young people some basic information about the range, scope, importance, and beauty of human sexuality.

In the past, books on sex education have generally been defective on the following three grounds:

- They treated sex in an abstract manner, as if it had little bearing on the personal life of the reader.

- They used highly complex terms without reference to their logical, psychological, social, and historical implications.

- Instead of the real human body they showed anatomical sketches, silhouettes, and schematic drawings, which often were reminiscent of blueprints or maps. In brief, they dehumanized sex by treating it as a mechanical process.

The present work tries to avoid these shortcomings and therefore uses a radically different approach:

- By providing specific and detailed information in hundreds of separate entries, the book is easily adapted to the personal questions of each individual reader.

- Furthermore, the encyclopedic format allows and, indeed, even calls for a careful definition of all terms, putting each of them in its proper historical and social perspective.

- Finally, the explicit photographs are not only instructive but also convey a much needed sense of joy, tenderness, and respect for the beauty and vulnerability of the human body.

The authors are well aware of the fact that it is unusual, perhaps even daring, to publish a book for young people with pictures that show "everything." The decision to do so does not stem from any desire to violate standards of decency, but to provide accurate visual information. It is common knowledge that young people today are more visually oriented than previous generations. Any attempt by educators to withhold from them a realistic pictorial presentation of human sexuality can only arouse their suspicion. Assurances that sex in itself is good and beautiful smack of hypocrisy as long as the frank presentation of all this goodness and beauty continues to be condemned and suppressed. It is for this reason that appropriate illustrations are indispensable for the success of sex education. As long as such illustrations are selected carefully and responsibly, their candor will not create but rather will prevent embarrassment on the part of both teacher and student.

However, sex education has to be more than uncensored factual information. Sex is not just a matter of biological facts, but of personal feelings, convictions, and habits, and these deserve the most careful consideration.

While no sensitive educator can afford to be dogmatic in these matters, he must nevertheless profess certain values on which to base his efforts. These are the fundamental values of all education: liberation from ignorance, fear, resentment, and superstition, and the cultivation of self-confidence and responsibility.

It is therefore only appropriate that a book such as this should place the facts of sex in their social perspective. There are for example specific entries referring to the past and present social position of women. Others deal with various movements for sexual emancipation. Special attention is also given to contemporary theological developments and the resulting changes in religious and moral concepts.

All of this is the legitimate concern of sex education. The authors of the present encyclopedia hope to contribute therefore not only to a better understanding of human sexuality but also to a greater awareness of its vast social implications.

How to use this book:

This encyclopedia is meant to serve two different, although equally important, functions:

- The alphabetical arrangement allows the reader immediately to find the answer to any particular question. Each entry is designed to provide a reasonable minimum of basic information.

- Each entry also invites further study by its various cross-references printed in **boldface**. Each of these **cross-references** represents a separate **entry** of its own which, in turn, usually contains new **cross-references,** thus providing the reader with an ever enlarging context for his initial question. In other words, the book can be used not only as a source of quick information but also as a permanent reference work for study and leisurely contemplation. This is more than merely a technical convenience: for notwithstanding its many advantages, the very structure of an encyclopedia might seem to lend itself to a fragmentation of knowledge. This would be particularly unfortunate in the area of sex.

Human life and human sexuality form a complex and mysterious whole whose innumerable, interdependent aspects defy any attempt by "specialists" to settle for definite answers. Indeed, it seems that, after all, sex is most appropriately seen in a religious perspective, as a God-given force which, although it might forever escape comprehension, is meant to lead us beyond ourselves to a realm of enduring love.

Martin Goldstein   Erwin J. Haeberle   Will McBride

aberration (or deviation) Specifically: sexual aberration or deviation. A term sometimes used to describe a **perversion.**

The use of the words "aberration," "deviation," and "perversion" is not entirely unproblematical. Occasionally, such terms are employed for moralizing purposes rather than for the benefit of scientific enlightenment. They imply certain value judgments that are not always made explicit. The terms "sexual aberration" and "sexual deviation" imply the existence of a "right" way of sex from which one can go astray; "perversion" implies that there is a "right" sexual drive that can be corrupted. However, the fact of the matter is that the criteria for "right" sex vary considerably from one time and culture to another. Even within one and the same culture, there are often wide differences of taste and opinion.

For instance, most people believed in the past, and many believe today, that only those sexual acts are "right" (moral) that serve the purpose of procreation. Consequently, any kind of sexual activity that, by its very nature, could not lead to pregnancy was considered "perverse" and an "aberration" (immoral). This blanket condemnation covered such varied activities as **masturbation, fellatio, cunnilingus, anal intercourse,** and **coitus interruptus.**

While most medical authorities today would no longer approve of this classification and its underlying assumption, some have replaced it with new value judgments of their own. For them, the only "right" (healthy) kind of sex is that which takes place between two members of different sex. Accordingly, everything that varies from this norm, such as **homosexuality** or **group sex,** is considered to be a sign of "perversion" or "aberration" (sick).

There are others who would subscribe to the same definition with the added restriction that "right" (normal and therefore legal) sex can only mean **genital** contact. Logically, they conclude that **oral** and **anal intercourse,** even between husband and wife, must be "perversions" and "aberrations" (abnormal and therefore illegal). This opinion is the basis of most **sex legislation** in the United States.

All three of these views are challenged as arbitrary and unscientific by still other authorities, and so the argument about the "right" kind of sex continues. The only way to resolve such disputes is by spelling out all underlying value assumptions, and by subjecting them to the test of critical rationality. (See also **deviant, unnatural sex.**)

abnormal
Different from the familiar, usual, and customary.

Some abnormal behavior may be indicative of physical or mental illness. However, this can be determined only by a professional diagnosis. In such a case, only professional treatment can help.

abortifacient
Medical term for a food, herb, liquid, chemical, drug or other agent which is believed to induce an **abortion.**

There is no oral medication known to induce abortion without harm to the mother. Supposed abortifacients such as hot baths or hot douches are also quite harmful and do not bring about the desired result. The same is true for physical self-abuse that is meant to lead to abortion, such as jumping up and down, lifting heavy weights, beating the stomach, or similar violent exercises. (See **unwanted pregnancy.**)

abortion
A term applicable to both the unintentional and the intentional premature termination of a **pregnancy.**

The unintentional termination of a pregnancy is called abortion if it occurs within the first 4 months; after that time it is usually called **miscarriage.** However, this distinction is not always strictly observed, and sometimes the terms "abortion" and "miscarriage" are used interchangeably.
The popular use of the term "abortion" normally restricts itself to the intentional termination of an **unwanted pregnancy,** an issue with numerous social, medical, legal, and moral implications.

An unwanted pregnancy can create many difficult problems. One of the most serious of these problems is the temptation on the part of the expectant mother to endanger her health and, indeed, her life, by desperate and ill-considered actions aimed at terminating the pregnancy. The real or imaginary difficulty of obtaining a legal abortion thus leads many women to experiment with useless, but quite harmful **abortifacients.** Others may consult criminal abortionists who often lack the professional skill or equipment to perform a medically safe abortion. Under these circumstances, an abortion can be a highly dangerous and degrading experience.

In recent years, many of the 50 states have liberalized their abortion laws with the result that today most American women should be able to have competent and safe medical abortions. Information about this possibility can be obtained from the local affiliates of **Planned Parenthood,** which also provide effective **birth control** help to avoid future unwanted pregnancies. However, since a number of states still retain their old, restrictive abortion statutes, many women may have to travel to another state in order to obtain a legal abortion.

It should also be noted that, according to certain religious views, abortions are immoral, because they involve the killing of a **fetus** or **embryo** which, for them, is a living, if unborn, human being. The Catholic church in particular considers an abortion to be murder, and many Catholic doctors therefore refuse to perform the operation unless the mother's life is clearly in danger.

abstinence
Avoidance of certain substances (such as foods or **drugs)** or of certain activities (such as **masturbation** or **sexual intercourse**).

Sexual abstinence can be the result of a voluntary decision, when for certain reasons a person decides that sexual activity is inappropriate at a given time or place. Abstinence can also be forced and involuntary (for example, in prison, army barracks, or hospital). Finally, sexual abstinence can stem from a conscious or unconscious **fear** of sex.

Our public morality demands sexual abstinence of all unmarried persons. One can safely assume that, on the whole, this moral demand cannot be, has never been, and is not now being met, because **sexuality** is an integral part of human life which cannot permanently be suppressed by public opinion or individual effort. Many young people experience personal conflicts as they do not know exactly how to use the period of adolescence for their sexual, personal, and social growth. There is no easy solution. Some people believe sexual abstinence to be the best preparation for marriage. Others admit that this is not true for everyone. However, adolescents who do not abstain from sexual activity can encounter considerable difficulties. (See **premarital sex.**) For **single** adults, and particularly for **homosexual** men and women, the official demand for their sexual abstinence also carries special hardships. (See **sex legislation.**)

In contrast to certain traditional religious views, many people today feel that the demand for sexual abstinence does not necessarily imply an abstention from masturbation, which they consider a kind of necessary safety-valve even for otherwise abstinent persons. Nevertheless, in the final analysis, this attitude amounts just as well to a denial of sex and its capacity for creating human contact.

The problems connected with voluntary and involuntary abstinence can be recognized and explained, if not totally eliminated, by professional guidance and counselling. In the future, our growing scientific understanding of human **sexual development** may alter social attitudes and regulations concerning abstinence.

acceleration
As compared to the last century, the physical and emotional development of teenagers has accelerated considerably. Today most 14-year-olds are taller than their ancestors of the same age were a 100 or even 50 years ago. It is also no longer unusual that boys and girls experience their first **ejaculation** or **first menstruation** at the age of 10. Generally, the **sexual development** of young people today presents a much less uniform picture than it did in the past. It is therefore more important than ever that generalizations about the physical ability and emotional **maturity** of adolescents be

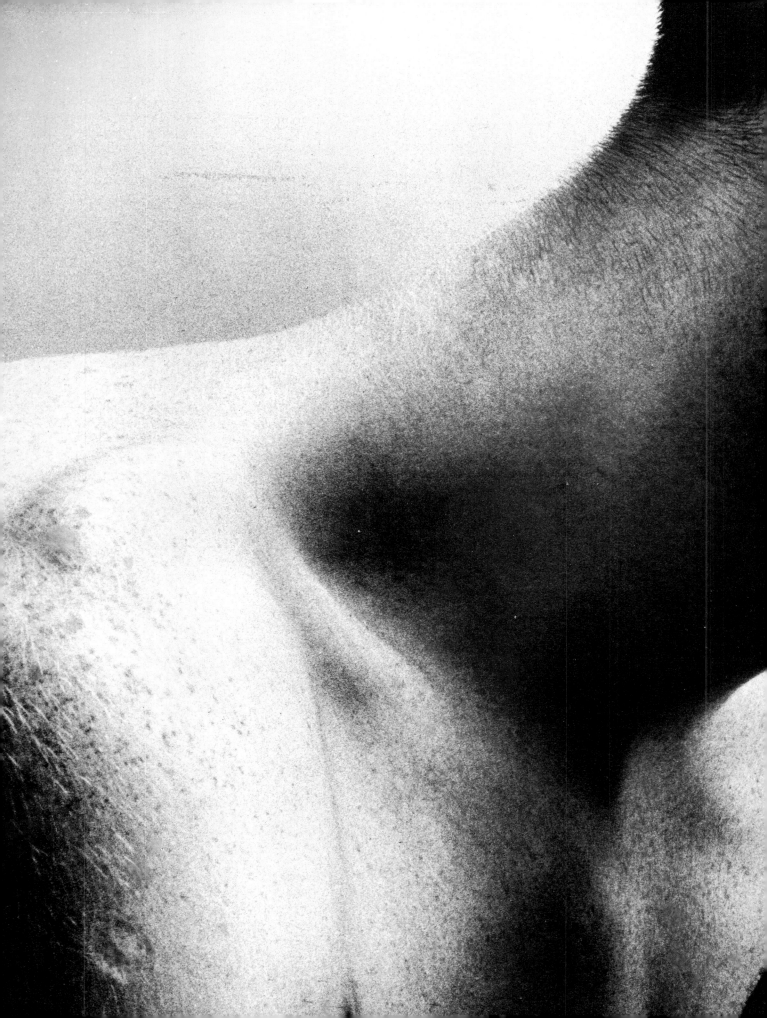

avoided. In this respect, each young person has to be judged individually. (See also **adolescence, minor**.)

acne

An inflammatory skin disease afflicting some boys and girls during **puberty.**

As a result of certain hormonal changes in the body, a number of small boils or pimples may appear on the skin of the face, chest, neck, and back. Although these pustules are basically harmless, they often become the source of self-consciousness, shyness, and embarrassment. However, a wholesome diet, fresh air, sunshine, and regular washing with soap and water can usually control the condition. In severe cases, acne can be alleviated by medical treatment, and, with the arrival of adulthood, it usually disappears altogether.
There is no connection between acne and sexual activity or inactivity.

Adam's apple

Colloquial term for the male larynx, which usually protrudes from the front of the neck. One of the secondary male **sexual characteristics.** (See **body.**)

adolescence

The period between the beginning of **puberty** and adulthood.

The phenomenon of adolescence, as we know it today, is the result of certain social and historical developments. Primitive cultures do not know an adolescence in the modern sense of the word, but use so-called puberty or initiation rites by which they confer the status of adults on their children as soon as these have reached a certain age. This means that, in these cultures, the period of transition from childhood to adulthood is extremely short. However, with the development and growing complexity of civilization, this transitional period gradually becomes longer until, as in many contemporary societies, it extends well over 10 years and more. It is not impossible that, in the future, the period of adolescence will last even longer.

As is obvious from this short sketch, adolescence is less a biological than a cultural phenomenon. In our culture, the main problems of adolescence seem to be the following:

- The adolescent tries to become materially and psychologically independent from his parents.

- He has to develop a sensible attitude towards his **sexuality** and towards sexual partners. (See **abstinence, masturbation, premarital intercourse.**)

- In many cases, he has to make up his mind as to whether he should continue his education or choose a profession or line of occupation, which may largely determine his future adult life.

- During this period, he also becomes concerned with questions about his own personal goals and ambitions and the meaning of life in general.

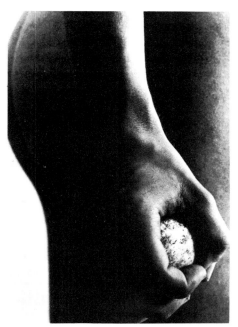

The difficulties of modern adolescence are compounded by the fact that the various goals towards which young people are expected to strive cannot be reached simultaneously. Physical maturity, intellectual balance, emotional stability, financial independence, and legal adulthood arrive at different stages of personal development.

As a result, young people usually find themselves torn between conflicting loyalties. The equal need for protection and independence can lead adolescents to seemingly contradictory actions and irrational behavior. These difficulties can be alleviated, if not entirely eliminated, with the help of understanding adults, who are honestly interested in the adolescent's personal growth. (See **emancipation.**)

During this period, a comprehensive **sex education** is of particular importance. The modern trend towards increasing **coeducation** can also contribute to easing much of the strain that is usually associated with the period of adolescence.

adultery

Sexual intercourse between partners of whom at least one is married to someone else. (See also **sex legislation.**)

According to certain religious views, all sexual relationships outside of marriage are considered adulterous, including not only **premarital intercourse** and **masturbation,** but even sexual desires, dreams, and fantasies of married partners which are not directed towards their own spouse. However, it seems more sensible to restrict the use of the world "adultery" to cases where certain acts or attitudes actually threaten an existing marriage. Such a threat can result not only from irresponsible sexual behavior, but also from other forms of neglect, egotism, and unfairness. Not only **extramarital intercourse,** but also **jealousy,** possessiveness, or insensitivity and lack of concern can ruin a marital relationship. A marriage can even be destroyed by a partner's obsession with his work or a hobby.

agape

A Greek term referring to a selfless, non-sexual **love** for one's neighbor. The greatest of the Christian virtues.

alimony

The payments that a husband has to make to his former wife after a **divorce**. Also the allowance payable in the case of a legal separation.

Alimony was once the exclusive privilege of women. However, in recent years, there have been cases where courts have ordered women to pay alimony to their former husbands. This is a sign of the growing **equality of the sexes.**

ambisexual

(adjective and noun) From Latin "ambo": both, and "sexus": sex.

Literally translated, the term means that the sex drive is directed towards persons of both sexes. An ambisexual is a man who falls in love with women as well as with other men, or a woman who falls in love with men as well as with other women.

ambisexuality

is the term used for the sexual disposition of people who are neither exclusively **heterosexual** nor exclusively **homosexual** in their responses.

In popular language, the terms "ambisexual" and "ambisexuality" are often replaced by the terms **"bisexual"** and **"bisexuality,"** a usage that can lead to confusion.

anal intercourse

Sexual intercourse by inserting the penis into the rectum (anus).

Since the rectum is normally one of the **erogenous zones,** many people enjoy anal intercourse. However, some others may vehemently reject it, considering it disgusting or dirty. In the final analysis, its appropriateness depends entirely on the judgment and understanding of the partners involved. Anal intercourse is not a **perversion.** Nevertheless, in most states of the USA it is illegal, even between husband and wife. (See **sex legislation.**)

anilingus

Licking of the rectal opening.

The rectum is usually one of the **erogenous zones,** and some men and women therefore engage in anilingus, either as a **foreplay** to **anal intercourse,** or for its own sake as one of many possible forms of intimate physical contact. There are people who have strong personal reservations against anilingus, just as against **cunnilingus** and **fellatio.** However, these sexual practices cannot be considered **perversions.** Their ultimate evaluation depends entirely on the attitude of the sexual partners involved.

aphrodisiac

(After Aphrodite, the Greek goddess of love) A substance believed to increase sexual desire and **potency.**

No foods, drinks, or chemicals can increase the capacity for love, or restore it where it has been impaired, or create it where it has failed to develop. However, it is possible to influence a person's physical reactions. There are, for instance, special diets that can build general physical strength and endurance. There are also certain substances that can increase blood circulation. This, in turn, may facilitate an **erection.** Alcohol can reduce or remove emotional inhibitions. Certain **drugs** can heighten a person's sensory perception or alter the state of his consciousness. Such effects may indeed help some people to establish sexual contact or to deepen their sexual experiences. Certain foods, such as eggs, oysters, celery, some spices, and some vitamins, are also supposed to stimulate the sexual drive. However, all of the ingredients believed active here are also part of our normal diet, and it is doubtful that an increased dosage would have any noticeable effect. Equally uncertain is the effect of additional male or female **hormones.** Temporary **abstinence** can occasionally build up sexual energies and, for a time, result in increased sexual activity.

The most obvious and effective aphrodisiac is an attractive sexual partner. His or her body, talk, gestures—in short, the partner's individuality and love—are the strongest stimulants for sexual desire. They are also the basis for a continuing, rewarding relationship. The entire range of

behavior that sexual partners develop towards each other contains innumerable stimuli which act as aphrodisiacs, and which give each sexual relationship its particular character.

Some people have also coined the term "anaphrodisiac," meaning a substance that reduces or even eliminates sexual desire. However, such substances have never been shown to exist. Nevertheless, there are now and then rumors that anaphrodisiacs are added to food in prisons or army barracks in order to keep the men quiet and docile. This rumor is probably caused by a fear among many men that their sexuality is being controlled by higher forces or authorities. Although such attempts may have existed in the past, their effectiveness has never been established, and can not be proven today. The most likely reason for this persistent fantasy is a harsh and repressive education. Its negative effects can continue to haunt even adult men and prevent them from emancipating themselves from emotional domination by their parents.

artificial insemination

A simple procedure in which a doctor injects male **semen** into a woman's **uterus** by means of a fine tube.

Artificial insemination is sometimes performed in cases where a married woman fails to conceive because of certain malfunctions of her sexual organs or the **impotence** of her husband. There are also instances where the sperm-cells of an otherwise sexually potent husband lack the strength to reach the female egg. Artificial insemination may also be considered by couples in certain cases of involuntary separation, since sperm can be preserved and stored in so-called "sperm banks."

The sperm used in artificial insemination, which is gained by **masturbation**, is usually that of the husband. However, if he is sterile, the sperm of an anonymous donor is used. (See **sterility**.)

asceticism

Renunciation of pleasure in favor of some special goal.

In a sense, we are all ascetics. Every life offers more possibilities than can be explored. Everyone has to restrict himself and constantly has to give up something in order to get something else. There is an inescapable, permanent, and occasionally frustrating necessity to make selections. In short, our lives are made up of innumerable individual choices according to some basic set of priorities.
In everyday language, however, the term "asceticism" is often used for the renunciation of comfort and luxury, or for **abstinence** from **sexual pleasure.**

asexual

(adjective) Non-sexual; without **sex**.

The term cannot really be applied to a person, since every man and woman is a sexual being. The word "asexual" does, however, provide a useful description of kinds of behavior which do not have or which seek to avoid any overt sexual implications.

For example, there is an asexual way of describing human reproduction by concentrating on the biological facts without reference to the feelings of the man and the woman involved. However, a thorough discussion of male-female relationships should also deal with the physical and psychological aspects of their **sexuality.** On the other hand, there will always be asexual relationships between men and women, such as professional cooperation at work. In fact, the ability of both sexes to engage in asexual relationships for the sake of some objective social goal is indispensable for the functioning of society.

autoeroticism A term sometimes used for **masturbation.**

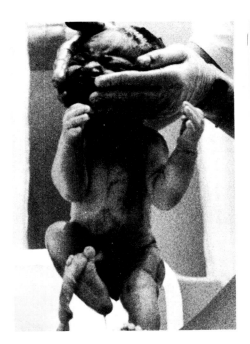

basal temperature See **rhythm method.**

bastard An **illegitimate child.**

The word "bastard" was once a neutral term which could be used in normal conversation. In the meantime, however, it has degenerated into a highly derogatory and offensive term, which is now often used without regard for its original meaning.

On the other hand, depending on the context, the word "bastard" can also become almost a term of endearment ("the poor bastard").

bestiality Sexual intercourse with animals. (See **perversion.**)

bigamist A person who is married to two people at the same time.

bigamy is the term used to describe this kind of marriage arrangement. It is illegal in the United States as well as in most other countries, **monogamy** having become the only accepted form of marriage.

birth The birth of a child occurs approximately 9 months after its conception. (See also **pregnancy.**)

The beginning of delivery is signalized by repeated labor pains which are caused by contractions of the **uterus** and which usually keep recurring over a period of several hours. At first, these contractions (each of which lasts about one half to one minute) occur at intervals of half an hour, but, as labor progresses, the intervals gradually become shorter until the contractions can be felt every one to two minutes. The labor

21

contractions first dilate the uterus, the cervical canal (see **cervix**), and the **vagina,** and finally expel the **fetus.**

Except for unusual cases, the baby is delivered head first. If the hands or buttocks appear first, the help of a physician is required. As soon as the baby is born, it begins to cry. This is a sign that its lungs have begun to function. Immediately after birth, the baby is still connected with the mother by the umbilical cord. This cord extends from the baby's navel to the placenta, the organ through which the fetus is fed. The umbilical cord has to be tied and cut. After the delivery of the child, labor contractions decrease in intensity, but continue until, about 20 minutes later, the placenta with the rest of the umbilical cord (the so-called afterbirth) is expelled. At the end of the birth, both the mother and her baby are exhausted and need rest.

Many husbands prefer to remain with their wives throughout the entire process and many modern hospitals encourage them to do so. (See also **natural childbirth.)**

birth control

The term "birth control" implies the ability of sexual partners to plan or prevent a pregnancy as a result of their sexual intercourse. In most cases, however, the term is used only in its negative, preventive sense, meaning a method of **contraception.**

There are several contraceptive methods:

- The **rhythm method,** or periodical sexual abstinence during a woman's fertile period. This period is determined either by mathematical calculation based on the length of menstrual cycles ("calendar method") or by a careful observation of the basal temperature ("basal temperature method"). The rhythm method is both complicated and unreliable. It is, however, the only form of birth control approved by the Catholic church.

- **Coitus interruptus.** This is the simplest birth-control method. It is well known and widely used, since it requires neither preparation nor supporting devices. However, it is unreliable and likely to put a physical and emotional strain on the sexual partners.

- The **pill.** The birth-control pill contains synthetic hormones which prevent ovulation. As a consequence, there is no egg, and fertilization is impossible. The pill is safe and reliable and offers the additional advantage of not interfering with the actual performance of coitus.

- **Diaphragm** and **cervical cap.** These contraceptive devices for women are inserted into the **vagina,** where they mechanically block the sperm from reaching the egg. They are fairly safe when used together with a spermicidal jelly.

- **Condom.** A contraceptive device for the male. The condom fits tightly over the erect penis and prevents the sperm from entering the vagina.

- **Spermicides.** These are chemicals which are introduced into the vagina, where they kill the sperm. Spermicides are often used together with either the diaphragm or the condom.

- **I.U.D.** Intra-uterine devices are small, mechanical birth-control devices which are inserted into the **uterus,** where they prevent pregnancy. There is still no satisfying explanation of how they work.

- **Sterilization.** Voluntary sterilization of men (**vasectomy**) and women (**tubal ligation**) is, in a way, the most effective way of birth control. However, since its results are irreversible, this method is appropriate only in a limited number of cases.

The various contraceptive methods mentioned above are aimed at preventing an **unwanted pregnancy** and at eliminating the need for abortions. An **abortion**, the artificial termination of a pregnancy, should not be considered a method of birth control, although the term itself would justify such an interpretation. (After all, an abortion does prevent a birth.) However, such usage can only further complicate an already complex issue. In order to avoid misunderstandings, the term "birth control" should therefore be replaced by "contraception," "conception control," or "pregnancy control." Unfortunately, it seems unlikely that such a change in terminology will be widely accepted within the near future.

As for the future of contraception itself, there are at present several research developments that could produce new chemical and hormonal contraceptives. The most important of these are:

- The "morning-after pill." This pill could be taken up to several days after coitus. It would prevent any fertilized egg from being implanted in the uterus.

- A "contraceptive vaccination" could produce antibodies which would destroy the sperm's fertilizing quality.

- Small "contraceptive capsules" could be deposited under the skin, where they would gradually release their contraceptive substance into the bloodstream. The capsules could thus remain effective for months or even years.

Eventually, it may also become possible to choose the sex of a child.

The invention of the birth-control pill has greatly stimulated the public discussion of contraception. It should be remembered, however, that most contraceptive methods known today have existed for a long time. The fact that they have remained so much less popular than the pill calls for an explanation.

One possible reason is the hesitancy of many people to touch their own genitals. The pill eliminates the need to do so. In fact, it seems to be entirely unrelated to the sexual act, while other contraceptive devices, such as diaphragm, cervical cap, and I.U.D., require a manipulation of the genitals. Condom and spermicides even have to be applied immediately before or during sexual intercourse itself. However, the aversion against this application often seems unnecessarily strong as a result of a prudish education. To some extent, the popularity of the pill may also be an expression of male supremacy, which prefers to leave men free and unconcerned at the expense of women. A contraceptive method which fulfills all demands for sexual equality has not yet been found. (See also **reliability of birth control methods.**)

Nevertheless, the recent progress in the area of birth control has been remarkable. However, there are still many people who manage to evade the issue by pointing to moral dogmas, medical controversies, and practical problems of application. Furthermore, in many cases, contraceptive devices are not even accessible. Young people in particular are often unable to obtain even the simplest birth-control information. In many countries, advertisements of birth-control devices are illegal. These facts are sufficient proof that there is still a great deal of resistance, fear, and even open repression in an area that is of vital importance to every sexually mature person.

The main reason for these difficulties is the fact that a wholehearted acceptance of birth control gives sex a new meaning. Throughout man's entire history, sex and procreation were inseparable. Sexuality was linked to parenthood, and parenthood to marriage. As soon as this traditional link is broken, sexuality, parenthood, and marriage acquire entirely new dimensions. There is a new freedom of action, which means a new need for personal choices, decisions, and responsibilities. The challenges of this unprecedented situation cannot be met by prohibitive ethics, restrictive laws, or repressive policies aimed at protecting the people against themselves. On the contrary, both the young and the old must be actively encouraged to develop the capacity for self-determination and to make good use of their new possibilities.

Unfortunately, there is still much controversy in regard to the use of birth control by young people and adolescents who, at least officially, are still expected to lead a life of sexual **abstinence.** (See **premarital intercourse.**) Many people continue to feel that sexual intercourse can be justified only by procreation. Thus even married men and women feel embarrassed when discussing the issue with others, or when asking for contraceptives in a drugstore. This persistent uneasiness results from a general **prudery**, which even pervades many attempts at **sex education.** While most sex educators have little difficulty explaining the biological facts of pregnancy and birth, many of them still feel uncomfortable when talking about birth control, because they then have to describe sexual organs and sexual activity.

On the other hand, there are now many qualified agencies, such as the **Planned Parenthood** offices, which openly offer birth-control services to all who seek it. Many college clinics have also begun to make birth control available to young, unmarried students. In view of these developments, the "protection of minors" from birth control seems justly doomed to failure. Eventually, all methods of birth control will have to be made available to all sexually mature persons, including young people.

bisexual
(adjective and noun) The term refers to the fact that every human body shows certain characteristics of both sexes.

bisexuality

is the word used to describe the basically bisexual predisposition of every human being.

In a human **embryo** the organs of both sexes are discernible, and a determination of sex is impossible at that stage. It is only during the later stages of its growth that monosexuality is established. However, slight remnants of the opposite sex remain even then. For example, every man has nipples just like a woman (although only a woman can produce milk), a woman's **clitoris** is the equivalent of a man's **penis,** and the body of each man and each woman contains both male and female hormones.

A person's **masculinity** or **femininity** is, to a large extent, defined by social influences on his or her development. Because of certain negative influences during childhood, some people are unable clearly to identify with either the masculine or feminine role. These people can often be helped by professional treatment. (See **sexual roles, transsexualism.**) In some very rare cases, a baby is born with both male and female sexual organs. (See **hermaphrodite.**)

Occasionally, the terms "bisexual" and "bisexuality" are used as synonyms for **"ambisexual"** and **"ambisexuality."** This usage can lead to confusion.

body

The sex of the human body is determined from the moment of **conception.**

At **birth** the baby's sex is recognizable only by its **genitals.** The external genitals (the **penis** in boys, the **vulva** in girls) are sexually excitable even in infancy. (See **erogenous zones.**)

During the second decade of life, the body accelerates its development and the sex glands (the **testicles** in boys, the **ovaries** in girls) begin to function. (See **puberty.**) Due to the influence of sex **hormones,** the secondary **sexual characteristics** begin to appear:

In females, the hips become wider than the shoulders, **breasts** develop, and **menstruation** begins.

In males, the shoulders become wider than the hips, there is a change of voice, the first **erections** and **ejaculations** occur, the beard begins to grow, and the larynx protrudes from the front of the neck. (See **Adam's apple.**)

In both sexes, pubic **hair** begins to grow around the genitals, **acne** may develop, the awareness of one's own body increases, and there is greater need for sleep. After puberty, the growth of the body comes to a halt, the bones lose their former elasticity, and there is a gain in weight and physical strength.

The human body as a whole, not just the genitals, is the vehicle for human **sexuality.** Sexual **excitement** and **desire** not only have psychological aspects, but also provoke strong bodily reactions. Indeed, all positive and negative emotions and impulses related to the **sex drive,** such as **love** and **tenderness** or aggression and **fear,** find expression in physical terms.

25

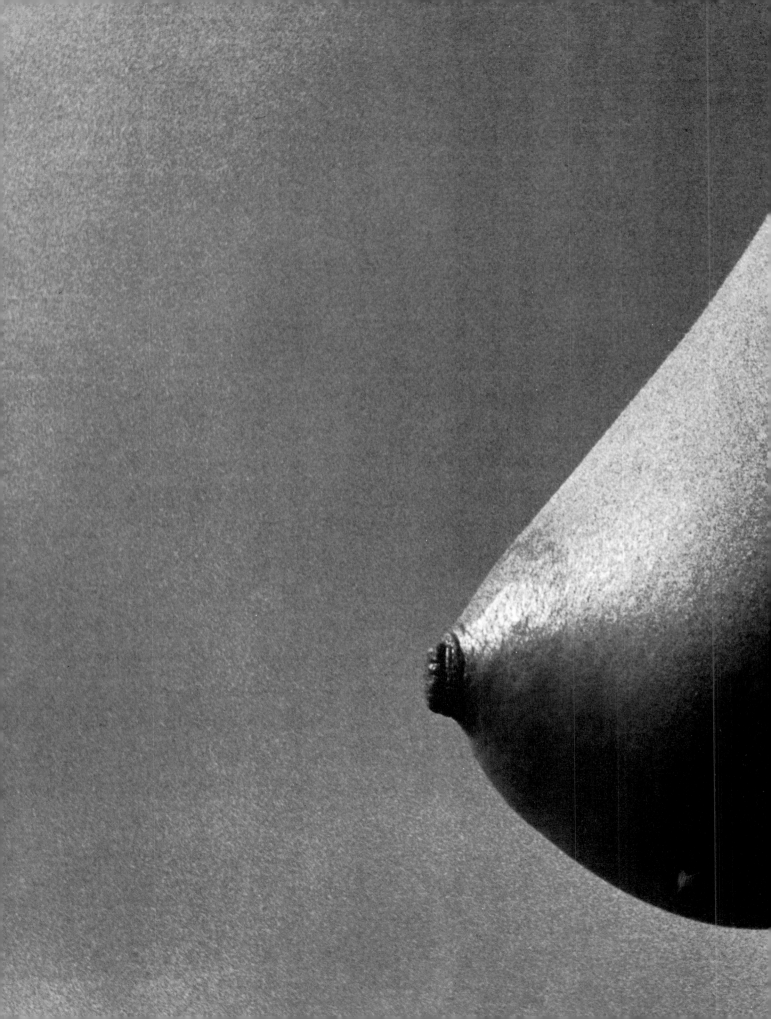

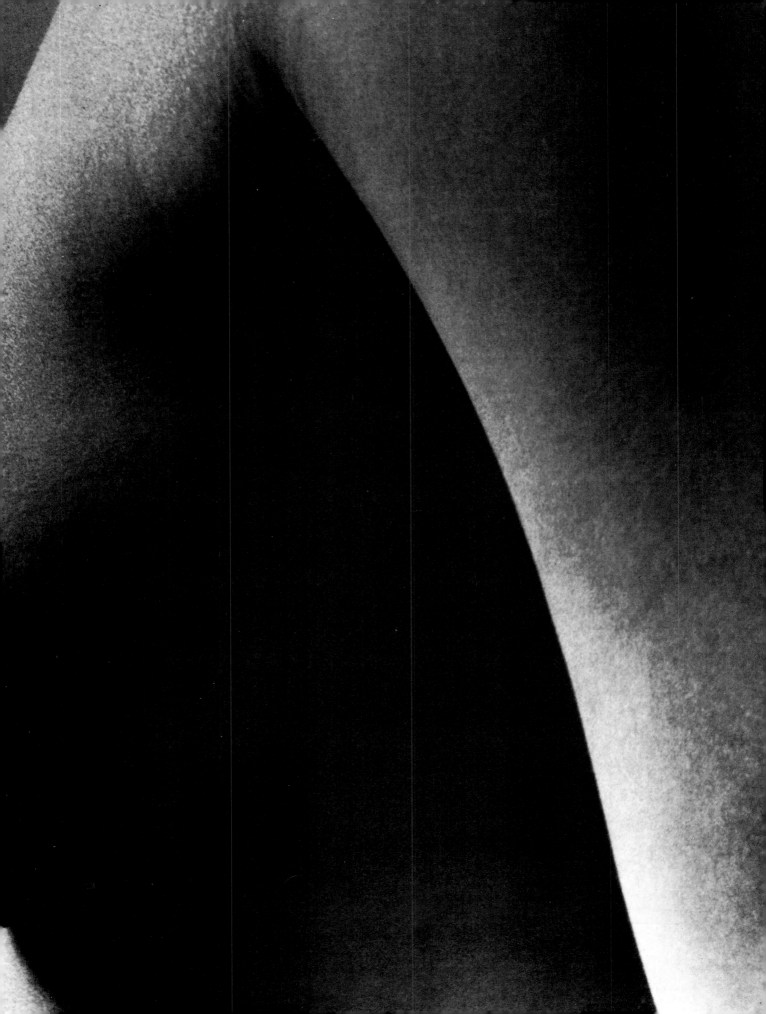

breasts The cushions of fat and tissue around the two mammary glands of a sexually mature woman.

The breasts belong to the secondary **sexual characteristics** of the female body, and they begin to develop during **puberty.** At the same time, the nipple at the tip of each breast becomes very sensitive to the touch. (See **erogenous zones.**) During a woman's **pregnancy,** her breasts begin to enlarge, and after she has given **birth,** they produce milk for the nursing of the baby.

Opinions about the ideal size or shape of the breasts vary from one time and place to another, and often even from person to person. Since the sight of a woman's breasts can cause or increase sexual **excitement** in men, their open display in public is usually discouraged as **obscene.** However, public reaction to such exposure is by no means uniform. This is evident not only from various female fashions, but also from the recent increase of so-called "topless" bars and restaurants in parts of the United States.

bride Traditional term for a girl or a woman on her **wedding** day.

bridegroom Traditional term for a man on his **wedding** day.

brothel A house where people can rent sexual partners for money. Men and women who sell their sexual services are called **prostitutes.**

Prostitution is illegal in many countries. Nevertheless, some of these countries have tolerated the existence of brothels in the past and continue to do so today. One exception is the United States, where brothels were formerly common, but have now practically disappeared due to increased public sensitivity and stricter law enforcement. As a consequence, prostitution in America has developed new organizational forms, such as that of the **call girl.**

The existence and the extent of prostitution are indications of the fact that many people are sexually unsatisfied, either because they are **single** and cannot find suitable partners, or because they are married but unhappy with their spouses. Prostitutes, because they are paid, are also often willing to satisfy **abnormal** sexual desires. In the past, there was a widespread belief that young men should learn sexual intercourse from prostitutes. This attitude was an expression of the sexual **double standard.**

buggery An old-fashioned term for **anal intercourse.** Like "sodomite" and **"sodomy,"** the words "bugger" (from Bulgar) and "buggery" are now becoming obsolete.

calendar method See **rhythm method**.

call girl
A female **prostitute** who can be called for a date by phone. The call-girl system is a modern form of **prostitution.**

carezza
(or "coitus reservatus") A form of sexual intercourse during which the man and the woman remain motionless for a long time, as soon as the penis has entered the vagina.

Some women experience several orgasms this way, while men do not try to reach, and generally do not have an orgasm. Instead, they derive satisfaction from the prolonged duration of the sexual union. Since there is no ejaculation of male sperm, carezza has sometimes been recommended as a method of birth control. It is obvious, however, that this method demands a great deal of self-control from both partners.
The practice of carezza originated with a certain religious sect whose members put a great emphasis on the union of souls.

Casanova
Name used to describe a man who devotes his life to the courtship of women.

Giovanni Jacopo Casanova was an 18th-century Italian adventurer who, in his memoirs, gave a very frank account of his many love affairs. He truly worshipped women, and few were able to resist him. Although he never tied himself to one woman for long, he felt regret at every separation. Many readers have been fascinated by Casanova's memoirs. His experience seems to prove that continuous courtship and seduction make the relationship between men and women more exciting. (See also **Don Juan.**)

castration

Removal or loss of the sex glands (the **testicles** in men; the **ovaries** in women).

A castration results in **infertility** and causes a number of other physiological and psychological changes because of the lack of sex **hormones.** However, it is possible to make up for this loss to a certain extent by hormone injections, although fertility cannot be restored.

The surgical removal of the sex glands is sometimes necessitated by injury or disease. Castration should not be confused with **sterilization.** It is not certain that a castration reduces, redirects, or eliminates the **sex drive.** (See also **eunuch.**)

celibacy

The state of being unmarried for professional or institutional reasons.

The term is most often used in connection with the fact that Roman Catholic priests and members of most religious orders take a vow to remain unmarried and to lead a life of sexual **abstinence.**

The institution of celibacy has recently come under attack by critics who see in it an expression of sexual **fear** and a flight from sexual responsibility. For them, celibacy has become obsolete as a condition for the priesthood. The defenders of celibacy, on the other hand, argue that only sexual **asceticism** enables a person to devote his full energy to social and spiritual matters. However, modern scientific findings indicate that a satisfying sexual relationship does not have to detract a man from his professional duties, but can, in fact, heighten his commitment.

cervical cap

A mechanical means of **birth control** similar to a **diaphragm,** but smaller and more difficult to apply. The cervical cap can be inserted only by a doctor, which greatly complicates its use. On the other hand, it has the advantage of being able to remain in place for up to a month at a time.

cervix

The neck of the **uterus.**

chastity

An attitude of sexual responsibility resulting in concern and respect for the sexual partner, treating him as an individual in his own right, not as a sexual object to be used at convenience. A chaste person is considerate and sensitive to the sexual needs, hopes, and fears of others.

Unfortunately, today most people equate chastity simply with sexual **abstinence.** This one-sided interpretation has robbed the word "chastity" of its original relevance, and has given it the appearance of old-fashioned narrow-mindedness.

childhood

The human **sex drive** already manifests itself in infancy and childhood. However, during infancy, the **genitals** do not yet play the decisive role in obtaining sexual gratification. Nevertheless, infants of both sexes experience pleasure from the stimulation of their genitals and other so-called **erogenous zones.**

Generally speaking, infant **sexuality** is still diffuse. Small children have no sense of **modesty** and no sexual **inhibitions.** They openly express interest in their own genitals and those of adults and remain undisturbed by the sight or smell of excrement. The **incest** taboo is not yet effective. On the contrary, small children are openly in love with their parents, seek their close physical contact, kiss and embrace them, climb into their bed, and want to marry them. (See **Oedipus complex.**) Only gradually, under the influence of their own experiences and the reactions of adults, do children adjust to their gender role or, in other words, find their own sexual identity. (See also **sexual development.**)

child molester

Lay term for a person, usually a male, who suffers from pedophilia, a sexual **perversion.** (See also **sex offender.**)

circumcision

Surgical removal of **foreskin** from **penis.**

Traditionally, Jews, Muslims, and many African peoples have circumcised boys in compliance with their religious laws and traditions. Among other religious groups or nations, circumcision of boys or adult men has also occasionally occurred for medical reasons when the foreskin proved too tight, inflamed, or infected.
In the United States today, circumcision has become general practice, with the result that almost all American boys are circumcised at an early age, usually at birth, thus avoiding possible later complications. However, it is debatable whether, apart from this preventive aspect, circumcision has any substantial positive or negative significance. It definitely does not, in anyway, influence the sexual abilities.

climacteric

Menopause. Change of life resulting from the gradual extinction of the reproductive capacities.

In women, the climacteric, which extends over a period of several years, usually begins towards the end of their fourth decade. It brings the gradual cessation of the menstrual flow and, finally, **infertility.** There may also be a number of other physiological and psychological changes. The sexual (as distinct from the reproductive) powers are not necessarily affected by the climacteric.
According to some medical opinion, there is also a climacteric in men, which supposedly begins at the end of their fifth decade. However, there is no doubt that the resulting changes, if indeed they occur, are less pronounced in males.

clitoris

Part of the external female **genitals,** situated at the upper frontal part of the **vulva** where the **labia minora** (inner lips) meet.

The clitoris is an organ which can be of different size in different women (usually one-fifth of an inch). It consists of erectile tissue and is partly covered by a **prepuce.** The clitoris belongs to the **erogenous zones,** and it can become erect during sexual **excitement.**
The clitoris is important for a woman's experience of **sexual pleasure** and **orgasm.**

coeducation

Education of boys and girls together in school and college.

In the past, students were usually separated according to sex. Female students generally received an inferior education and were entirely barred from colleges and universities. After the industrial revolution, and with their growing **emancipation,** women have gradually won access to higher education. Today most institutions of higher learning are coeducational.
Nevertheless, even now much of what passes for coeducation is actually no more than co-instruction. In other words, male and female students are offered the same courses and may sit in the same classroom together, but lead otherwise totally separate lives. However, true coeducation aims at a common educational experience for boys and girls who approach and solve their personal problems together and also share their recreational activities. The goal of this kind of coeducation is the universal cooperation between the sexes. Obviously, this goal can be reached only if the educators themselves are men and women who cooperate on the basis of full equality. (See **equality of the sexes.**)

coition

Coitus.

coitus

Sexual intercourse between man and woman by inserting the **penis** into the **vagina.** The subsequent mutual movements of both partners lead them to increasing **sexual pleasure,** and finally to **orgasm** and sexual **satisfaction.** Under certain conditions, coitus can lead to a **conception.** (See **fertility, rhythm method.**)
Coitus is by no means the only form of sexual intercourse, although it is perhaps the most common. It can be performed in various coital **positions.**

coitus interruptus

Interrupted **sexual intercourse.** The man withdraws his **penis** from the **vagina** before **ejaculation.** This is a simple and common, if crude form of **birth control.** However, the method may prove ineffective if the sperm comes in contact even with the external female genitals (**vulva**). Sperm cells, once ejaculated and in contact with a mucous membrane, can move by them-

selves, and are capable of wandering through the vagina and reaching an **ovum,** thus causing pregnancy. It is also possible that small amounts of sperm leave the penis before ejaculation. In view of these facts, coitus interruptus is not reliable as a method of birth control. Furthermore, it is emotionally unsatisfying for many people. It can also have a negative effect on the over-all relationship between sexual partners, because the need to control the sexual reactions at all times creates physical and emotional tensions.

coitus reservatus
Medical term for **carezza.**

commune
In recent years, the shortcomings of the **nuclear family** have led many young people to experiment with communal living arrangements.

A commune is a modern form of the **extended family** and usually consists of several married and single adults and their children who pool their financial resources and share a house or an apartment. In some cases, the individual members retain their own rooms and their personal privacy. In other cases, they may develop a closer relationship, which may even include some form of **group sex.**

Not all experiments in communal living have been successful, since thus far few people have been able to develop the necessary democratic lifestyle. The advantages of a commune are: a considerable reduction in living expenses, more free time, and increased financial and emotional security for its members. It is likely therefore, that these experiments will continue in the future, and they may eventually lead to a new, workable family structure.

conception
Beginning of **pregnancy.**

A conception occurs when the ripe **ovum** is fertilized by one of the **spermatozoa** during **coitus.** This fertilization takes place inside the **uterus** or one of the **Fallopian tubes.** (For fertilization without coitus, see **artificial insemination.**) As a result of its fertilization (see also **zygote**), the ovum develops into an **embryo** and later into a **fetus.**
A conception is possible only during a woman's fertile period. (See **rhythm method.**)

concubine
A woman who lives with a man in a relationship of **free love** and who, therefore, does not enjoy the social and legal privileges extended to a wife. (See **marriage.**)

condom
(also called "contraceptive," "prophylactic," or "rubber") A **birth control** device for the male.

A condom is made of thin rubber and is shaped like the finger of a glove. As it fits tightly over the **penis,** it prevents the sperm from entering the

vagina. While a condom provides some protection against infection with a **venereal disease,** it is not completely reliable as a means of birth control. (See **reliability of birth control methods.**) However, careful application can increase its effectiveness.

For example, when a condom is used, some space should be left at the tip of the penis in order to accommodate the **semen** after ejaculation. Otherwise the condom may burst. Semen may also be spilled into the vagina when the erection of the penis subsides while still inside of the vagina, or when the condom slips off upon withdrawal.

There are also special condoms which increase the size of the penis, or which have a rough or irregular surface in order to provide greater vaginal stimulation (so-called "French ticklers"). In some cases such condoms may be an appropriate means to improve a sexual relationship. However, they cannot truly eliminate sexual problems arising from emotional disorders.

continence   A word sometimes used for sexual **abstinence.**

contraception   Literally, the prevention of a **conception.** The term is used for methods or policies aimed at the avoidance of pregnancy.

In recent years, the once popular word "contraception" has gradually been replaced with the less precise term "birth control." (For further details see **birth control.**)

contraceptive   See **condom.**

conventions   Social rules intended to facilitate relations between people by imposing certain limits on the spontaneous actions and expression of the individual.

Conventions change, and sexual conventions are no exception. For a long time, men have enjoyed certain privileges denied to women. (See **double standard.**) The custom, for instance, that a man orders a woman's food in a restaurant, and picks up the check, has its origin in the fact that formerly women were not allowed to appear alone in public, and did not possess any money of their own. Traditional sexual conventions also implied that women were sexually passive and unable to experience **sexual pleasure.** The same conventions discriminated against unwed mothers and their children, and prevented early and proper **sex education.** Furthermore, they demanded that children and adolescents should not engage in any sexual activity, but practice total sexual **abstinence.**

It is also a matter of convention that men dress differently from women and have different hair-styles.

There can be no tolerable social life without certain conventions. However, in the future, such conventions are likely to be more diverse and subject to faster change. The individual man or woman will less and less be able to fall back on existing conventions, but will find it necessary to be more creative and invent new, appropriate social rules for new social situations.

copulation
Physical union of **penis** and **vagina.** (See **coitus.**)

crime against nature
A legal term referring to certain kinds of sexual behavior. (See **sex legislation.**)

To a modern layman this usage may appear strange and peculiar, since the words themselves seem to suggest something else. Indeed, it would appear that the term would be more appropriate for water- and air-pollution or other destructive acts that ruin man's natural environment and upset the ecology. However, this particular legal term dates back to the Middle Ages, and the word "nature" has here a very different, rather mystical meaning which is inaccessible to modern science and even ordinary common sense. (See **unnatural sex.**)

crush
Colloquial term for a sudden and intensive emotional attachment to another person.

Crushes are particularly frequent during **adolescence,** when boys and girls may develop close **friendships** with members of their own sex, or may fall in **love** with members of the opposite sex, sometimes with persons much older than themselves. This kind of emotional attachment does not necessarily involve sexual desire.

A teenager's **first love** may seem unreasonably exclusive and unrealistic to outsiders (if they should happen to become aware of it), and the teenager himself may be unable to understand or control his emotions. An adolescent who falls in love for the first time tends to project his own image of an ideal partner on the beloved person who therefore appears surprisingly familiar and trustworthy. He seems to fulfill the lover's every desire to be understood and cared for. This impression, however, is unlikely to be permanent. Usually, the feelings lose their intensity with time, and the relationship then turns into a less emotional friendship. Occasionally, such a youthful crush can even lead to a later **marriage,** although this is quite rare. In any event, it implies a change in the nature of the attachment. In other instances, the infatuation ends suddenly, like a dream, and no explanation for the former feelings seems possible. (As long as they lasted, no explanation was needed.)

Whenever we find that our love has died, we should not conclude that the experience was worthless, or that the formerly adored person was really undeserving of our attention. On the contrary, only after we have fallen in love several times can we gain the experience that is needed to appreciate our partners fully. This experience can also help us to avoid hasty decisions (such as a sudden marriage, for example).

People who are in love should meet and get to know each other. Thus they will find out whether they are indeed compatible and whether they can have a future together. In this sense, every crush can contribute to a deeper understanding of all factors involved in personal attraction between people. This, in turn, will contribute to a person's emotional **maturity.**

cuckold Term for a husband whose wife has a lover. A traditional literary and theatrical motive.

Many classical comedies show the artful cunning of wives who deceive their unloved husbands, thus making them objects of ridicule. The dramatic stereotype of the aging cuckold was an expression of the popular opinion that impotent and insensitive husbands had no right to the **fidelity** of their wives. This opinion belongs to a time when marriages were arranged by the couple's families, most often without regard for the bride's own interests and wishes.

cunnilingus Licking or sucking of the female genitals. As with **fellatio,** this is a common form of sexual activity.

The appropriate form of sexual intercourse depends entirely on the judgment and the mutual understanding of the partners involved. Many women enjoy cunnilingus, as it heightens their sexual pleasure. Cunnilingus is not a **perversion.** However, in most states it is illegal, even between husband and wife. (See **sex legislation.**)

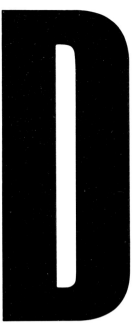

dating Meeting by appointment of unmarried males and females for the purpose of socializing or as a form of courtship.

In many parts of the United States, dating is an established custom which often follows an almost ritualistic pattern. This custom serves several useful functions:

- It helps young people to find contact with others and strengthens their self-confidence in relation to members of the opposite sex.

- It develops a sense of courtesy and good manners.

- It facilitates the selection of a partner for **marriage.**

Like most **conventions,** the custom of dating is subject to change. An increasing number of teenagers today do not care to repeat the more formalized dating patterns known to their parents, but prefer more spontaneous meetings and associations. Indeed, it cannot be denied that the traditional form of dating had a number of undesirable features, and that in many cases it took on competitive aspects for social "success" that resembled a popularity contest. Instead of contributing to a better understanding between the sexes, it often led to a disregard for the dating partner, whose availability thus became a means to some egotistical end. In the future, the increasing **coeducation** of boys and girls in high school and college may well contribute to the development of new, meaningful forms of dating.

defloration Rupture of **hymen.** The act of depriving a girl or a woman of her **virginity.**

Traditionally, the only appropriate occasion for a woman's **first sexual intercourse** was her **wedding night,** when her husband expected to find her hymen intact as proof of her premarital sexual **abstinence.** (See also **double standard, petting.**) However, there have been primitive cultures in which a girl's hymen was incised by a priest as part of the initiation rites. A secularized version of this custom survived until about 200 years ago in certain parts of Europe, where the feudal lords reserved the right to deflower the brides of their serfs. (See **jus primae noctis.**)

Although the rupture of the hymen may cause some slight bleeding and discomfort, there is no need for a woman to fear any great pain. Men, on the other hand, ought to remember that the first **coitus** should be preceded by some sort of **foreplay** or **petting.** The first insertion of the **penis** into the **vagina** should be attemped slowly and without force, and it can be facilitated by stretching the hymen with the fingers and by the use of a **lubricant.**

desire
More specifically: sexual desire. The wish to be loved and sexually satisfied or to engage in sexual activity. (See also **excitement.**)

deviant
A person whose behavior differs from the socially accepted norm. A sexual deviant is somebody whose sexual behavior differs from the sexual standards of his society. As these standards vary, so does deviance. What is considered deviance at one time and place may be accepted behavior at another time and place.

Originally, the word "deviance" implied a going astray from some "right" path of life. Today the scientific use of the term no longer carries this implication. Nevertheless, in order to avoid possible confusion among laymen, it is sometimes advisable to replace "deviance" with "variance," which has never had any negative connotations. (See also **aberration.**)

deviation
Specifically: sexual deviation. See **aberration.**

diaphragm
A safe, cheap, and fairly effective mechanical means of **birth control** for women.

The diaphragm is a small bowl-shaped device made of soft rubber which is placed inside the **vagina** covering the **cervix.** As a result, the sperm entering the vagina during **coitus** is mechanically blocked from reaching the **uterus.**
In order to increase its effectiveness, the diaphragm is normally used together with a spermicidal jelly. (See **spermicides.**)

The diaphragm is available only on prescription, since it has to be properly fitted by a doctor, who also has to instruct the woman in its use. Given the proper instruction, the woman can later insert the diaphragm herself.
The diaphragm is inserted before each **coitus,** and must not be taken out until 8–12 hours after the last **ejaculation.** However, it should never remain in its place for more than one day. After removal, it is cleaned with soap and water and can be used again.

dildo
An artificial **penis** made of plastic, rubber, or wood.
There are also penis-shaped electric vibrators on the market which are used by some women for the purpose of **masturbation.**

dirty books   See **sex books.**

dirty joke
The so-called **obscene** or "dirty joke" is an expression of secret or unfulfilled sexual desires. It relieves psychological tensions arising from the necessity to repress certain sexual wishes, or to avoid sexual topics in normal conversation. (See **monogamy.**)

"Dirty jokes" (and certain graffiti on toilet walls) provide a kind of safety valve for sexually frustrated individuals who thus express their forbidden thoughts and fantasies. Consequently, the prevalence and the content of "dirty jokes" in any given society are often related to the number and character of its **taboos.**

dirty pictures
Colloquial term for pictures that show nudity or sexual activity. (See **obscene, pornography.**)

Formerly, such pictures (the so-called "French postcards") were privately and secretly imported from European and Latin American countries. Today, in a climate of growing sexual tolerance, they appear in special magazines or are sold as single prints or slides in special stores ("dirty bookshops").

divorce
The legal dissolution of a valid **marriage.** (A divorce has to be distinguished from an annulment, which is the declaration by a court that the marriage was void from the beginning.)

In the United States, each state has its own divorce laws, which differ not only in regard to the legal grounds for divorce, but also in regard to residence requirements. It is therefore impossible to give an adequate account of these laws within the scope of the present volume.

Since modern marriages result from the free personal decision of two individuals, there is also the possibility that, at a later date, they may arrive at a change of mind when one or both of them find themselves disappointed by the institution of marriage or by their particular marriage partner. However, the consequences of a divorce can be more of a problem than the divorce itself, and, if a marriage should never be taken lightly, neither should a divorce. In some instances, a **marriage counsellor** can help the marriage partners in identifying and solving their marital problems and thus prevent a divorce. In other cases, however, the preservation of an unhappy marriage may do more harm than good. In any event, it is very important for the partners involved to learn how to cope with their basic problems in order to avoid them in the future.
One reason for marital difficulties that can lead to divorce is the modern family form. (See **nuclear family.**)

The Catholic church does not recognize divorce, as it considers marriage to be indissolvable (except by death). However, under certain conditions, a special church court may declare an annulment.

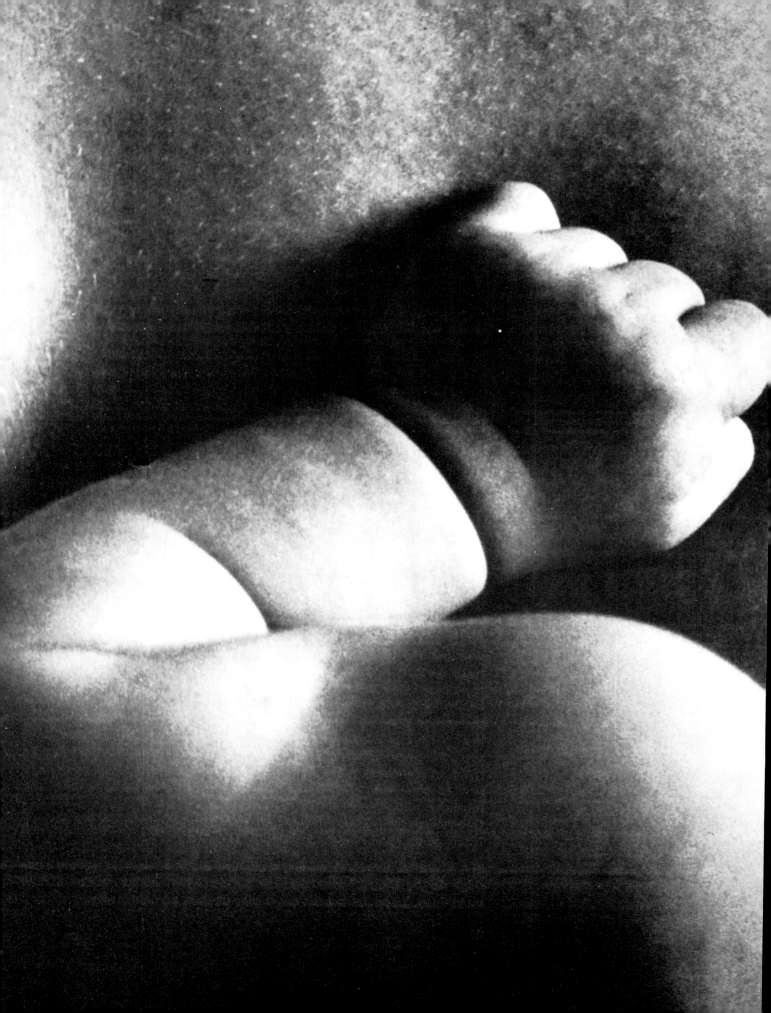

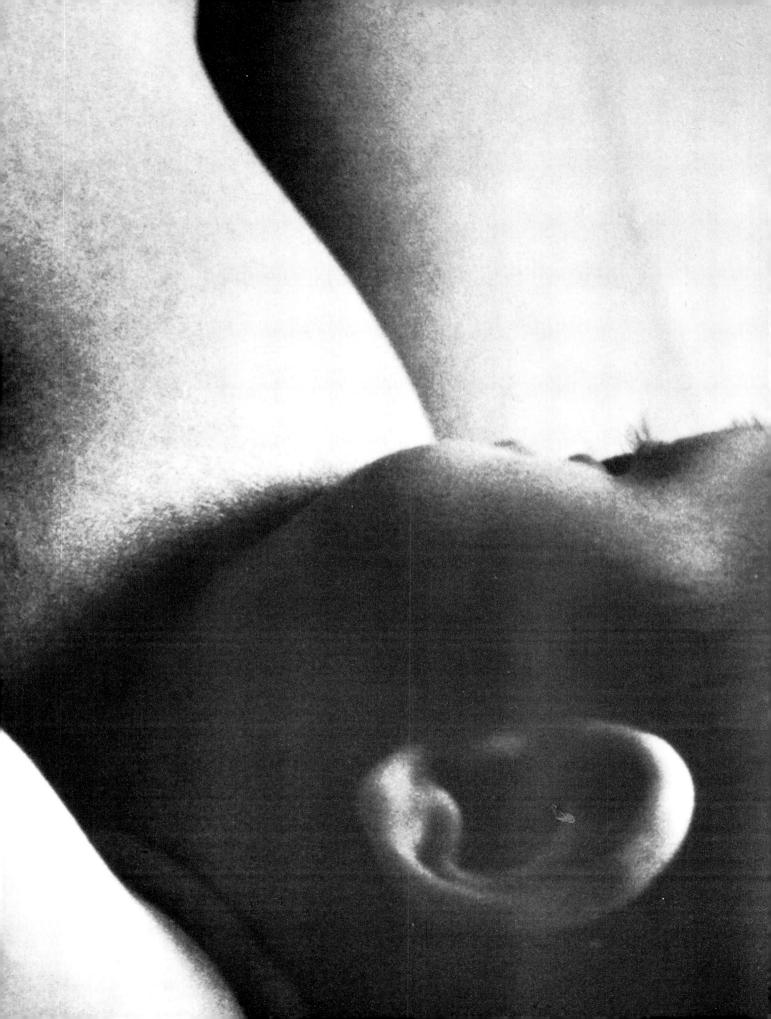

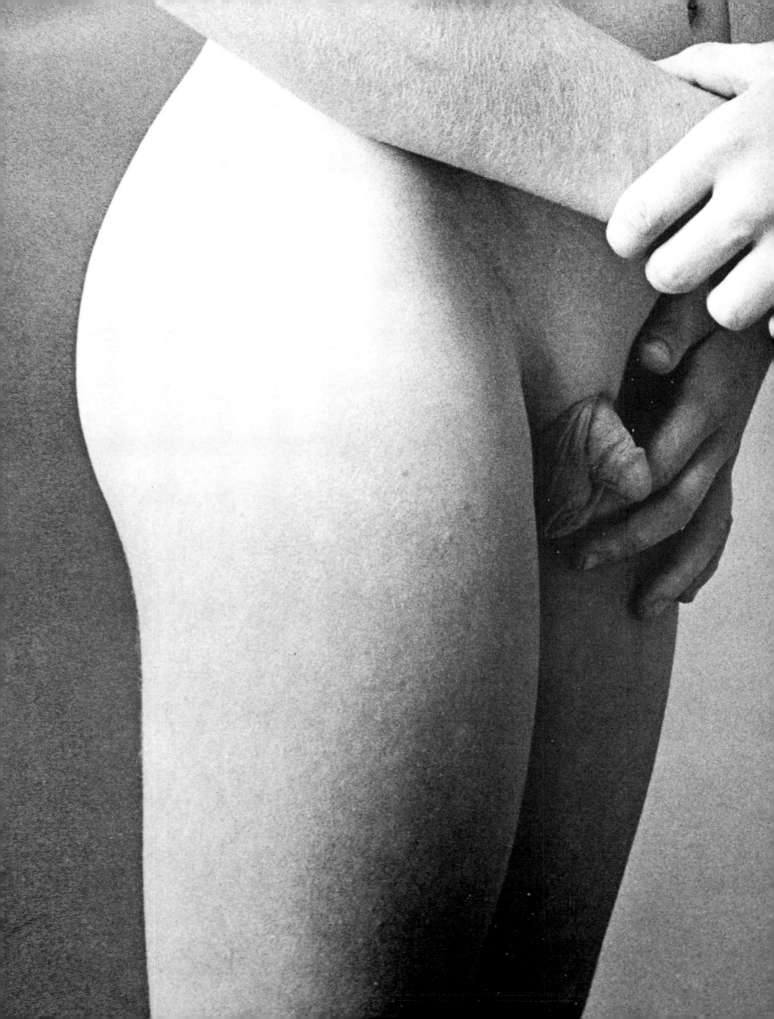

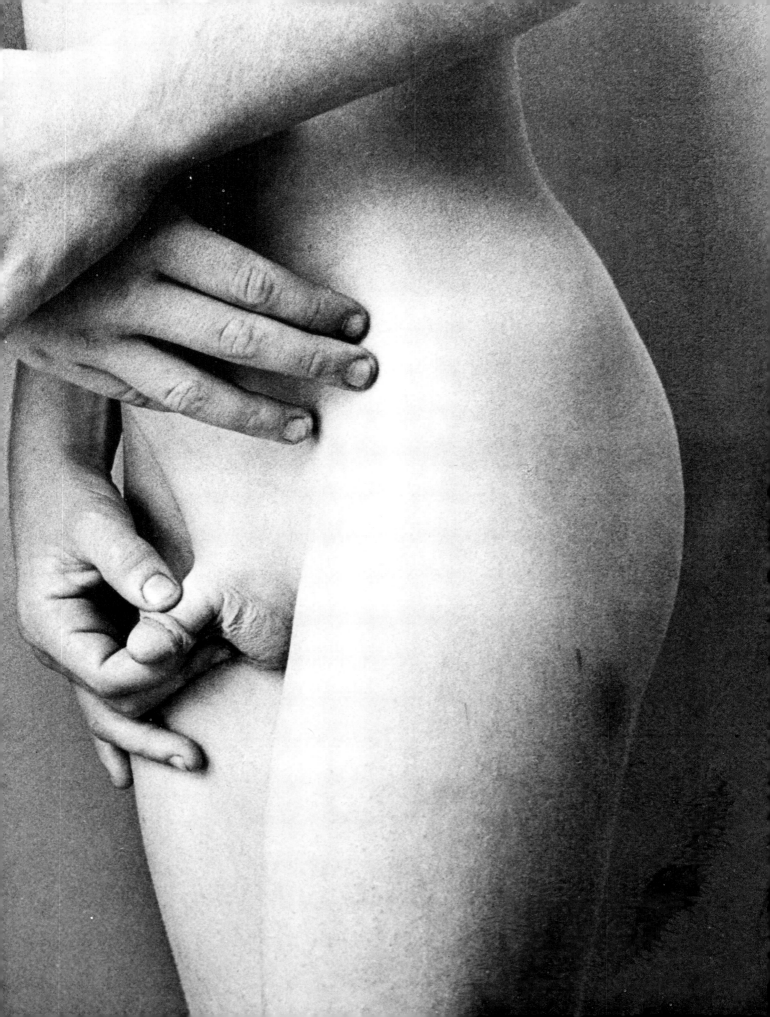

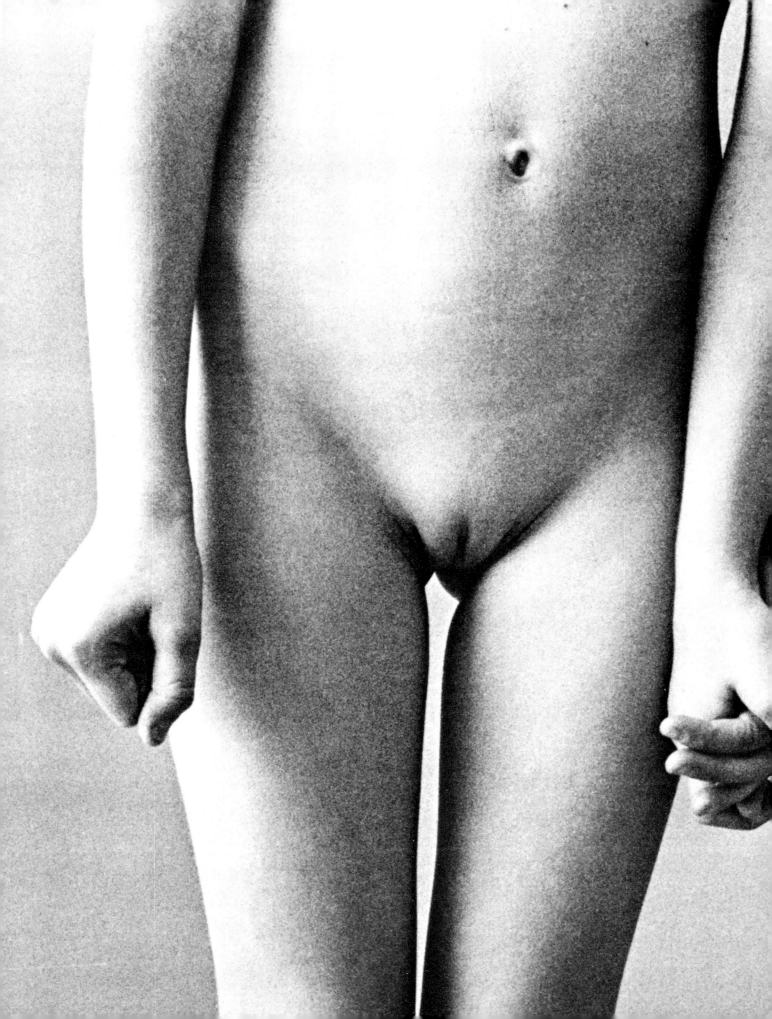

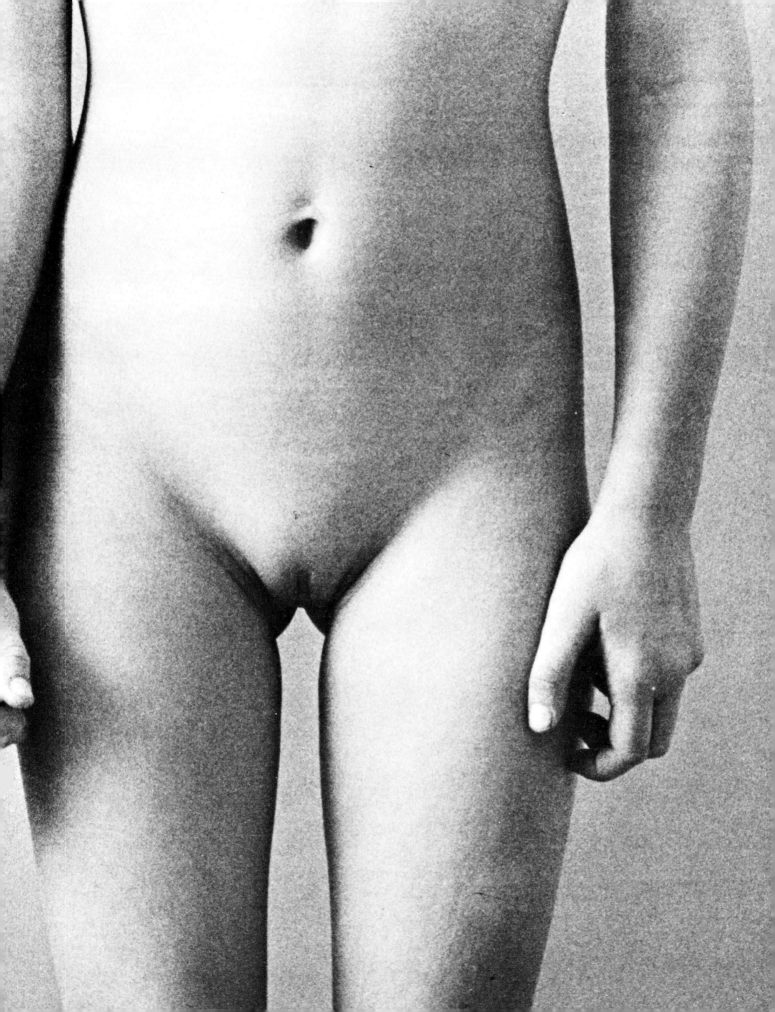

dolce vita

(Italian: "sweet life") A term used to describe a life of pleasure.

"La dolce vita" is the opposite of the normal working life, which is ruled by discipline and sexual restraint. It is an old dream of mankind to "escape from it all" and lead a life of happy indulgence. As this proves impossible for most people, they try to capture at least a glimpse of it during their vacations, or they nourish their fantasies by reading about the "beautiful people" who supposedly lead a never-ending "sweet life."

Don Juan

A compulsive seducer.

The character of Don Juan was created by the Spanish playwright Tirso de Molina (d. 1648). Since then, the figure of Don Juan has continued to inspire various works for the theatre, of which the most famous are Molière's comedy "Dom Juan" and Mozart's opera "Don Giovanni."

In contrast to the historical character of **Casanova,** the legendary Don Juan is interested only in sexual conquest. As soon as he has seduced a woman, he abruptly loses all interest in her. Don Juan is unable to establish any lasting personal relationship, but is obsessed with the need to "prove his **masculinity.**"

double standard

Specifically: sexual double standard.

Traditionally, society has demanded that women conform to a standard of sexual behavior different from that of men. While **premarital** and **extra-marital intercourse** for women has been universally condemned, men have generally been granted considerable license. (See **patriarchy.**)

Although essentially illogical and hypocritical, the double standard has nevertheless sometimes been defended with pseudo-arguments such as: "men are naturally polygamous," or "women become emotionally fixated on their first lover," or "a man has to be able to awaken a woman's slumbering sex drive." All of these contentions have been disproved. However, it seems that only the full **emancipation** of women will succeed in erasing the last traces of the sexual double standard. (See also **prostitution.**)

drugs

In our society today, the term "drugs" is most often used in reference to chemical substances that alter mood, perception, or consciousness.

The best known of these substances are alcohol, cannabis (marijuana and hashish), opiates (heroin, morphine, opium), barbiturates ("downers"), amphetamines ("uppers" or "speed"), and hallucinogens (mescaline, LSD).

People take these drugs for a variety of motives. In most cases, however, the basic reason for prolonged use is some feeling of discontent, frustration, inadequacy, uselessness, boredom, anxiety, or depression. Drugs seem to offer a means of escape from such unpleasant moods and from the circumstances that breed them. However, this escape is never more than temporary, and many drugs, in fact, create more difficulties than they could ever have been expected to solve.

Certain drugs pose a serious health hazard. Furthermore, a number of them are illegal in the United States, and they can be obtained and consumed only under the constant threat of arrest and conviction. In addition to these and many other complicated social, medical, legal, and moral problems that are connected with the use of drugs, there is also the possibility of drug-dependence. Alcohol, morphine, heroin, and barbiturates, among others, are potentially "addictive," that is, when taken in certain quantities, they bring about changes in the body of the user resulting in his dependence on continued use. The body establishes a "tolerance" requiring more of the drug to ward off painful withdrawal symptoms. As a consequence, the user's entire energy tends to become focused on the fight against the arrival of that "moment of truth" when he could find himself without the needed supply. (The "wino" and the "junkie" are typical examples.) The preoccupation with the next "fix," the growing inability to cope with or even consider any other problem, turns the life of such a person into a self-enclosed system, and he becomes incapable of establishing and maintaining meaningful personal relationships with others.

However, for some people, even the use of drugs that are not physically addictive in this sense may become a "habit" and create a kind of psychological dependence on their effects. In some instances, this kind of dependence can just as well result in emotional self-isolation and an impoverished, ever-narrowing outlook on life.

The serious problem of drug-dependence would not be eliminated by a legalization of all drugs. People who have become dependent on drugs invariably suffer from an inability to find true human contact. Once the drug has become the center of their lives, it serves as a substitute for all other pleasures, including **sexual pleasure.**

The healthiest "high" is sexual **excitement** and **orgasm**, and sex is the only "trip" that can lead to a fuller and more rewarding life. (See also **aphrodisiac.**)

ecstasy A state of extreme pleasurable excitement.

In a state of ecstasy, a person loses his self-control and expresses his deepest emotions through unconscious and involuntary sounds and gestures. At the same time, his sensual perception is partially impaired. Sexual **excitement** and **orgasm** are typical examples of ecstasy.

egg See **ovum.**

ejaculatio praecox See **premature ejaculation.**

ejaculation The sudden emission of **semen** from the **penis** during **orgasm.**

An ejaculation may occur spontaneously, as for instance in the form of a **nocturnal emission** ("wet dream"), or it may be brought about deliberately during **masturbation** or **sexual intercourse.** Boys experience their first ejaculation during **puberty,** usually between the ages of 11 and 13.

The semen discharged in an ejaculation consists of a blend of several secretions which are produced by the **testicles** and other glands. One ejaculation may contain several hundred million **spermatozoa.** However, the quantity of sperm-cells contained in the semen decreases with the man's age and with repeated ejaculations within a short period of time. This biological fact has led some men to the erroneous belief that they can avoid making a woman pregnant by masturbating before engaging in **coitus.** They thus hope to have exhausted their sperm supply long enough to allow for intercourse without release of additional sperm. Apart from the fact that, under these circumstances, sexual intercourse can become difficult and frustrating, this supposed method of birth control is so unreliable as to be virtually useless.

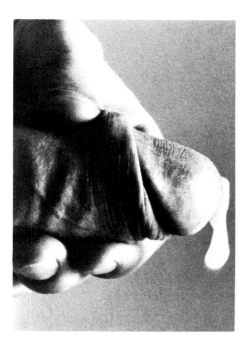

There is no need to fear that "too many" ejaculations could somehow weaken the body. In fact, an increase in the number of ejaculations may even stimulate the testicles to produce more sperm-cells. The number of possible ejaculations within a certain period of time varies from one individual to another.

Electra complex

See **Oedipus complex**.

emancipation

Liberation of oppressed groups of society, giving them equal rights with others and taking away the privileges of their oppressors. An oppressor in this sense is anybody who benefits (even unknowingly) from the legal inequality of others.

The most prominent example of sexual emancipation is the emancipation of women. In their long fight for equality women have, in time, won the following rights: the right to choose their own marriage partner, the right to learn a trade or a profession and to work in their chosen occupation, the right to higher education, the right to vote and to be a candidate for public office.

The emancipation of women, once completed, will mean the end of the patriarchal form of society. Men will have to share their powers of leadership and decision-making. Many men fear the emancipation of women, as they anticipate a decline in their own influence. They overlook the advantages which can result from increased cooperation and shared responsibility. (See **patriarchy**.)

Theoretically, the emancipation of women has been achieved in the United States. However, in practice, women are still treated unequally. Often they are paid less than men for the same work; they are promoted later and fired sooner than men, and they are discouraged from entering certain "male" professions. Consequently, there are few female surgeons, airline pilots, dentists, or ministers, although there is no convincing reason why women could not perform these jobs just as well as men. The general public attitude still expects women to find their true calling in being wives and mothers, and to assume a rather passive sexual role. However, the arrival of the birth-control pill has already shifted a certain amount of sexual responsibility and initiative to women.

Another example of sexual emancipation is that of **homosexuals** who, after a long period of oppression in many Western countries, have now begun to organize in order to fight public and private discrimination. In recent years, homosexual organizations have been opening up in many cities in the United States. These organizations try to educate the public on the subject of **homosexuality**, and to work for the legalization of all sexual acts between consenting adults in private (which would include homosexual acts). Apart from these formal organizations, there are also more informal groups devoted to **"Gay Liberation."** These groups consist mostly of students and are usually based on college campuses.

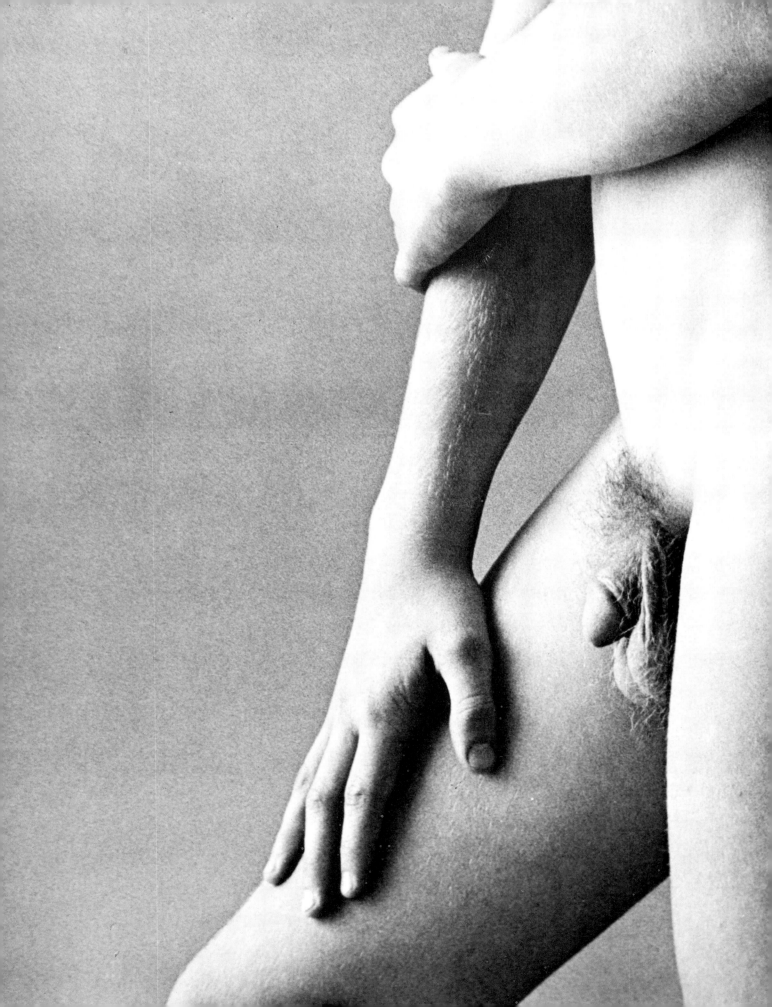

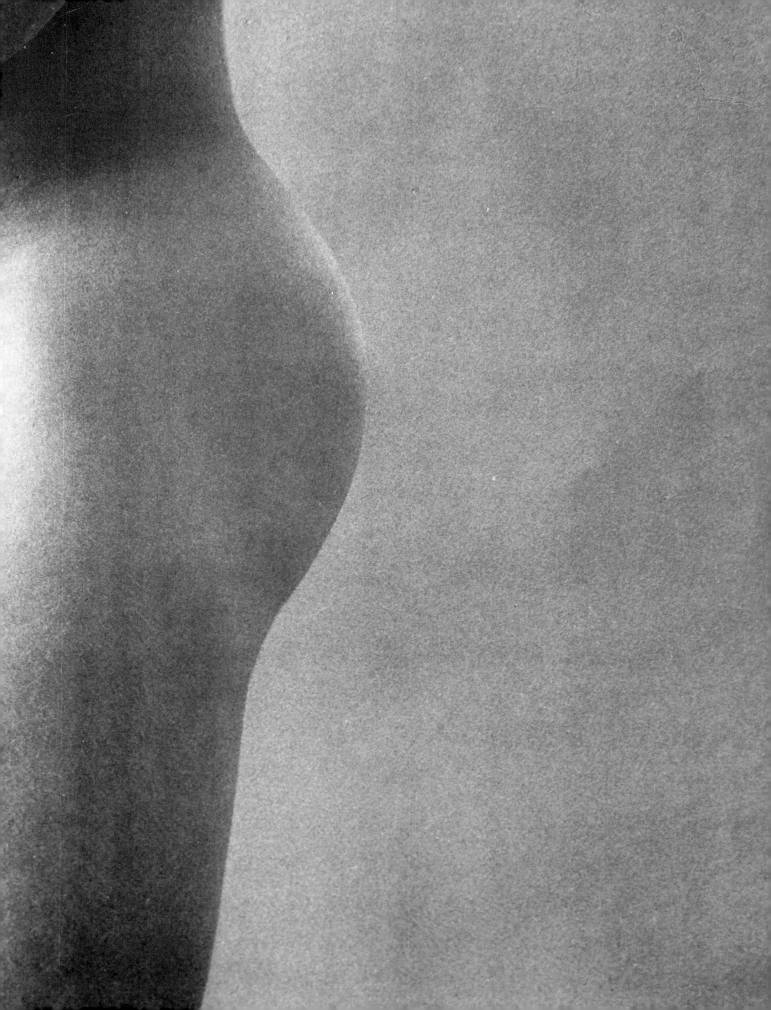

The essential demands of homosexuals for their civil rights and for freedom from persecution are today supported by most medical and legal authorities. During the last decades, this expert support has led to the repeal of anti-homosexual laws in such countries as Denmark, Norway, Sweden, the Netherlands, Great Britain, Canada, Switzerland, West and East Germany, Poland, Hungary, and Czechoslovakia. (The Catholic countries of Southern Europe and Latin America never had such laws.) In the United States, similar legal reforms have been recommended by the American Law Institute and by the National Commission on Reform of Federal Criminal Laws.

A third example is the emancipation of the young.
Although a 1970 Supreme Court decision has granted to 18-year-olds the right to vote in Federal elections, most young people are denied any decisive influence concerning their own lives. They have no control over their finances and are subject to numerous legal restrictions. As students, they have little or no influence on their education. Finally, as **minors**, they are also restricted in their sexual activities. (See **premarital intercourse**.)
The emancipation of young people aims at the abolition of authoritarian social structures, and at their participation in social decisions relating to their own lives. This goal can be reached only if young and old learn to cooperate on the basis of mutual understanding and respect for rational arguments. Adults will have to learn that authority must be earned, not just inherited. Young people, on the other hand, must recognize that increased participation means increased responsibility. The emancipation of the young is a difficult task, as it implies substantial changes in society, particularly in education. (See **sex education.**)

embryo Medical term for the developing baby during its first stages of life inside the mother's womb. Within three months, the embryo grows to a length of about 4 inches. After the third month of pregnancy, the unborn baby is called a **fetus**.

engagement Mutual declaration of intent by two people to marry each other. This declaration is often formalized by a public announcement.

Engagements were necessary at a time when men and women did not enjoy complete freedom in choosing their marriage partners, and when families, trade guilds, or other social institutions participated in their decision. Today, on the other hand, even parents are not always asked for their permission. Instead, often the engaged couple simply informs them of their decision. This is usually followed by some sort of family celebration at which the engaged couple receives presents. Then the actual preparations for the wedding begin.
Since the engagement as such does not, in any way, imply a change in sexual relations, in social standing, or in the living arrangements of the parties involved, it no longer serves an essential social function.

equality of the sexes

In virtually all societies, the biological difference between men and women has been used as the basis for assigning them different social roles. Although these roles may vary from one time and culture to another, they have usually implied a lower social, legal, and economic status for women. (See **conventions, double standard, father, patriarchy.**) In modern times, this state of affairs has increasingly come under attack by feminists who demand the **emancipation,** that is, the full legal equality of women.

Feminists justly resent the fact that, even today, many women who want to advance to positions of influence in our society have to play a masculine role. (See **sexual roles.**) The structure of the modern **nuclear family** also contributes to the persistent inequality of the sexes. As long as men remain the exclusive providers of their families, while women spend their lives as housewives and mothers, true sexual equality is impossible. Only when both husband and wife can work in their chosen profession and when both are financially independent and equally contribute to the support of their family will sexual equality have been achieved. (See also **sexual revolution.**)

Historically, Christianity has been one of the few religions to recognize and support the equality of men and women. Unfortunately, the organizational structures of the Christian churches, which even today are still patriarchal, have never reflected this revolutionary doctrine.

There should be no need to emphasize that the legal and social equality of the sexes does not mean an obliteration or abolition of biological differences. On the contrary, such equality would, for the first time in history, give both men and women an equal chance to develop all of their individual capacities and thus contribute not to greater uniformity but to a greater variety of human life.

erection

Swelling, stiffening, and rising of the **penis**, usually caused by sexual **excitement.**

The stiffening results from the fact that the hollow erectile tissue inide of the penis becomes filled with blood. A corresponding process can be observed in the female body, as the **clitoris** and the nipples of the **breasts** show an erection in response to sexual stimulation.
In the state of erection, the penis can be inserted into the **vagina** for the purpose of **coitus.** The inability to have an erection is called **impotence.** However, this condition is cause for concern only if it occurs repeatedly.

Boys normally experience erections consciously for the first time during **puberty**, although it is not unusual that even children have erections. (In these cases, there is, of course, no potential discharge of semen.) An erection is usually caused by erotic thoughts or sights, or by the touching of the **erogenous zones**. It can, however, also result from a variety of other causes.

erogenous zones

Certain parts of the body can, when touched by a sexual partner, cause or increase sexual excitement. These so-called erogenous zones are usually the following: the external genital organs, breasts, nipples, mouth (see **kiss**), rectum (see **anal intercourse**), and certain areas of the skin (face, neck, inside of thighs).

It depends very much on the individual and on the situation whether any or all of these erogenous zones develop their particular sensitivity. Only time and experience can make a person aware of his erogenous zones. Their response is never automatic. They stimulate sexual excitement only in situations of mutual sexual consent, and do not respond at all in cases of rape. On the other hand, new pleasurable sexual encounters can lead to the discovery of new erogenous zones and of their various responses to certain stimuli such as kisses, caresses, licking, rubbing, slapping, or tickling. Potentially, every part of the human body can be an erogenous zone.

Just as each individual is different from others, so are his reactions. For this reason, everyone has to find out by himself which parts of his own (or his partner's) body react as erogenous zones.

Eros

(Latin: Amor or Cupid) The god of **love.**

According to Greek mythology, Eros symbolized life and creativity. To be in love meant to be possessed by a divine force. This force caused people to long for beauty and excellence, not only in the physical world, but also in the realm of the spiritual. Man could love not only his sexual partner, his family, or his friends, but also his country, national heroes, or artistic ideals.

Although we still use the word "love" in all of these cases today, we see a great difference between such love and sexual desire. To us moderns, only the latter seems "erotic."

On the other hand, there are people who insist that there is a difference between the "erotic" and the "merely sexual." According to this usage, the term "sexual" refers exclusively to the "baser" biological needs, while the word "erotic" implies "higher" spiritual desires. (See **Platonic love.**)

Our everyday language has thus far failed to adopt this distinction. In fact, the word "erotic" is sometimes found to be more base and objectionable than "sexual." However, the exact meaning and effect of these and similar words depend very much on the context and on the cultural background of the speaker or listener.

erotic

(adjective) "Sexually stimulating," or simply "related to matters of **love** or **sexual intercourse.**"

erotica

(plural) Books, pictures, films, or records dealing with sexual matters. (See **sex books.**)

eroticism
A term with several meanings:

- A strong "sex appeal." (See **sexy**.)
- A cultivation or refinement of sex.
- A preoccupation with sexual matters.

erotomania
A constant, irrepressable sexual desire. (See also **nymphomaniac**.)

eugenics
"The study of forces under social control which enhance or impair the inborn qualities of future generations." Since heredity is governed by certain biological laws, it is possible to influence the result of the breeding process by selective mating. This is constantly being done in animal breeding. However, basically the same laws also apply to human procreation. While there is no compulsion for men or women to choose their marriage partners according to these laws, prospective parents can take advantage of modern genetic knowledge in order to avoid needless suffering. For instance, a person afflicted with a hereditary disease, such as hemophilia or certain mental diseases, may decide against having children of his own.

eunuch
A man whose **testicles** have been surgically removed before **puberty**.

This operation is called **castration**. As a result, the body fails to develop such typically male characteristics as a beard and a deep voice. The sex drive also remains underdeveloped.

The term "eunuch" is normally used only for harem guards in Islamic countries. However, the practice of castrating young boys was also known in 18th-century Europe. The so-called "castrati" (male altos) were then in great demand for the opera stage, and some of them became very rich and famous. The leading parts in the operas of George Frederick Handel, for example, were written for castrati. Since today this type of voice can no longer be provided, the operas are either rearranged for modern voices (tenor, bass) or left unperformed.

excitement
A state of tension, triggered by some experience or some recollection or intuition.

Sexual excitement, which is the most obvious physical and psychological expression of the **sex drive,** can be initiated by external stimuli such as sounds, sights, and the touching of the **erogenous zones** or by internal causes such as conscious and unconscious thoughts, dreams, and fantasies. In males, the most important physical symptom of sexual excitement is the **erection** of the **penis;** in females, the main symptoms are a swelling of the **vulva** and the increased lubrication of the **vagina.** Sexual excitement, just as any other state of excitement, impairs the ability for self-control. Certain **inhibitions** or sober intentions can sometimes be swept away by **passion.**

It is characteristic of the tension created by sexual excitement that it tends to seek relief through sexual activity leading to **orgasm,** which results in physical and emotional **satisfaction** and relaxation.

There is no universally effective technique that could produce or heighten sexual excitement under all circumstances. Each individual responds differently to different stimuli. Sexual partners should therefore not rely on any stereotyped approaches but try to be sensitive to each other's needs and desires. (See also **aphrodisiac, sex manual.**)

There is a general impression that men are more quickly and easily aroused than women, and that sexual excitement in males is primarily caused by stimulating sights while women need the personal reassurance of being touched. However, there is reason to believe that this difference in sexual responses (if indeed it exists) is not biologically determined, but is the result of educational influences.

In the absence of external or internal restrictions, sexual excitement leads to **sexual intercourse.** Under certain circumstances, **masturbation** can provide a substitute. However, since it lacks the element of human contact with others, it is, in the long run, bound to prove unsatisfactory as the only form of sexual activity.

exhibitionism   See **perversion.**

exhibitionist
A person, usually a male, who, in order to find sexual satisfaction, feels a compulsion to expose his genitals in public to strangers, often women and children. (See **perversion**).

An exhibitionist, although most often a sick person in need of medical attention, is usually criminally prosecuted as a **sex offender.**

The psychological harm done by an exhibitionist is frequently exaggerated by over-concerned parents and public officials. There is a fear that little girls might experience a shock at the sudden sight of a penis. However, such shocks do not occur where children are given early and proper sex education.

Certain exhibitionistic tendencies can also be found in some **strip-tease** dancers, or nude **go-go girls.**

extended family
A **family** consisting of more than one married couple and their children.

There are two types of extended family:

1. A household including several generations of one family (parents, children, grandchildren) plus various married and unmarried relatives (aunts, uncles, cousins) plus a number of domestic servants. In such a household, power is distributed unequally according to age, sex, and relation to the "head of the family."

For thousands of years this was the normal type of family. Its structure corresponded to the needs of a basically agrarian society. However, since the beginning of the industrial revolution, the extended family has gradually been replaced by the **nuclear family.**

2. A communal household of several adults and their children, intended to overcome the disadvantages of a nuclear family. Today there are various models for such communal living:

- The kibbutzim in Israel, where people share the means of production and are equally trained to join in their defense.

- Socialist communes, in which people share everything, and which often impose a great deal of conformity on their members.

- New communal living arrangements (also often called **"communes"**) in Western Europe and in the United States, where a number of married and unmarried adults and their children pool their material resources (or part of them) without surrendering their personal independence.

The advantages of the modern extended family are:

- Living costs are lower, because more people share the cost for food, rent, and appliances.

- There is a more democratic division of labor; privileges can be abolished.

- There is more intellectual and cultural stimulation.

- The individual enjoys a greater amount of emotional and economic security.

- The individual has more time for professional, social, and political activities.

- There are no "unwed mothers," and no "illegitimate" children.

Such modern extended families are still rare, and where they exist, they are still in a state of experiment. So far, only a few mature persons have been able to adopt the truly democratic life-style that these experiments require for their success. The final shape and structure of the modern extended family cannot now be predicted, although it is clear that it does not necessarily have to mean **group sex** and socialized property. However, there is reason to believe that the extended family, in one form or another, is the family of the future.

extramarital intercourse

Sexual intercourse outside of marriage.

The term is usually applied to married people who have sexual intercourse with partners other than their spouse. (See also **fidelity**.)
The term is inappropriate in connection with **single,** widowed, or divorced persons. (See also **premarital intercourse**.)

Fallopian pregnancy

(also called "tubal pregnancy" or "ectopic pregnancy") A pregnancy during which the fertilized **ovum**, instead of moving on into the **uterus**, attaches itself to the wall of one of the **Fallopian tubes**. This leads to the eventual bursting of the tube and to internal hemorrhage, requiring immediate surgery.

The remaining second Fallopian tube preserves the woman's ability to have other children.

Fallopian tubes

(named after Fallopius, the anatomist who discovered them) Oviducts. Two tubes connecting the **ovaries** with the **uterus**.

After **ovulation**, the **ovum** moves through the Fallopian tubes into the uterus, a passage that takes between 8 to 14 days. The fertilization of the ovum usually occurs inside the Fallopian tubes.

family

Social unit consisting of a married couple and their children. This modern definition corresponds to the social reality in most industrial nations, where the former **extended family** has been replaced by the **nuclear family**.

The extended family traditionally united several generations under one roof. The house, the land, and the family business passed on from father to son to grandson and provided the main element of stability, while the choice of individual marriage partners and the conduct of a particular **marriage** were of secondary importance. The survival of the family and the increase of its property were the primary goals to which every member was expected to contribute. More children meant more contributors to the family's wealth and power. Sons were particularly welcome as additional workers and defenders of the clan. They also insured the welfare of their parents during old age. Sex was a means to provide family continuity; potentially, all sexual acts served the purpose of procreation.

Today a wedding usually marks the beginning of something entirely different. A marriage may very well express the intent to found a new family; however, this family does not come into existence until after the birth of the first child, and it dissolves again when the adult children leave the house of their parents. In other words, marriage in the past took place within the larger framework of the family, while today the family is a passing aspect of marriage. Formerly, the family outlasted the marriage; now the marriage outlasts the family. This fundamental change in the family structure has also meant changes in human sexual behavior. Sexual intercourse now mostly serves to strengthen the personal relationship between marriage partners, and it leads to procreation only if and when they decide to have children. (See **birth control, woman.**)

The new family structure imposes new social roles on both men and women. The husband usually works outside of the home, while his wife is restricted to housekeeping and taking care of the children, who are now largely removed from the direct influence of their father. Nor is there any relevant family tradition to be carried on. Each generation makes a fresh start of its own. The family members are isolated from their more distant relatives as well as from their neighbors. At the same time, however, parents and children make greater emotional and material demands on each other. Consequently, there is a continuous need for discussion, planning, readjustment, and reorientation. Occasionally, the frustrations encountered by the nuclear family lead to **divorce**. Recently, there have also been more positive attempts to escape these frustrations by experimenting with new social forms such as **communes** or similar living arrangements comparable to the former extended family.

In the past, marital difficulties were usually resolved, or at least reduced, with the assistance of the various close and distant relatives who were members of the same household. In contrast, modern family problems sometimes require the help of outsiders such as **marriage counsellors** and other professional people. The nuclear family is also ill-equipped to provide the young with an adequate education, including **sex education**. Most educational functions have therefore been taken over by public schools and job-training programs. To a considerable extent, the care for the old and disabled has also been delegated to the state (Social Security, Medicare, Welfare). On the other hand, the family has retained certain psychological functions which have now become more important than ever. For instance, even the nuclear family can still offer an emotional shelter, a protected sphere, where people are valued for other reasons than success and performance. This is indispensable for any healthy **sexual development**.

family planning

A term summarizing the motives, goals, and actions necessary for a conscious and deliberate way of establishing and maintaining a family.
Family planning makes the timing of the first pregnancy, the size of the family, and the tempo of its growth subject to a conscious decision by both husband and wife. (See **Planned Parenthood**.)

However, family planning can also be seen in a larger context as a national, or even international, policy which influences the growth of families by certain tax deductions or medical and welfare programs.

The term "family planning" is also used as a euphemism for **birth control**, especially in connection with the attempt to restrict the use of contraceptive devices to legally married couples.

father For thousands of years, fatherhood was considered the final proof of manhood. The ability to produce offspring was vitally important for the survival of the **extended family**. The father, as the "head of the family," was its provider and protector, the source of its life and power, and he ruled over his wife (wives) and his children with absolute authority. This position of unlimited power also served as a model for the rule of emperors, kings, and dictators who called themselves the "fathers" of their peoples, and who claimed a father's authority not only over their own families, but over all families within their realm. The analogy was carried still further by the belief that an almighty "father in heaven" exercised the same absolute control over the "family of man."

Because of its underlying philosophy, this form of social organization has been called the "rule of the father," or **patriarchy** (from the Latin "pater": father).

Although our society today is still largely dominated by patriarchal values, it has, in the meantime, undergone several substantial factual changes. The rule of kings, for example, has been replaced with more democratic forms of government, and the former extended family has been reduced to the **nuclear family**. This new family form, however, can operate and survive only on the basis of shared responsibilities which must, eventually, lead to the legal **equality of the sexes**. This, in turn, will redefine the concepts of fatherhood and motherhood. (See **mother, woman**.)

Because of these modern developments, it has become difficult for many men to play the role of father. In many cases, they simply do not have enough time for their children, who now often have to grow up without a father-figure whom they can follow. (See **Oedipus complex**.) But even if a father can find the time, he is often uncertain about his educational task. When he himself was a child, the world was very different from today, and in order to help his children fit into the world of tomorrow, which will be even more different, he can hardly follow the example of his own father. Obviously, in the modern, fast-changing world, authoritarian rule can no longer provide successful guidance into the future, but has to be replaced by partnership. It is therefore necessary that father and mother develop a relationship of equality, mutual trust, and cooperation, which then will also be able to include their children.

62

fear Specifically: sexual fear. Many people are afraid of sex. Symptoms of this fear are: excessive modesty, an all-pervading bad conscience and constant anxiety, unreasonable **inhibitions,** and the painstaking avoidance of sex, even as a subject of conversation. (See **prudery.**)

Sexual fear in an individual can become so overwhelming as to cause physical discomfort and even illness. Society in general expresses this fear in its far-reaching, detailed, and severe **sex legislation**, in prohibitive **sexual ethics**, and in violent opposition to **sex education**. However, it is the lack of proper sex education that causes the fear in the first place. As it stands, the public is extremely touchy and uneasy in sexual matters. There is a widespread belief that sex is something inherently dangerous and dirty. For many people sexual activity is accompanied by feelings of shame and guilt.

Sexual fears cannot be overcome by simple appeals to courage ("Show me that you are a man," or "Don't be silly"). Nor can the problem be solved by benevolent exhortations ("That's quite normal," or "Just stop worrying about it"). These tactics often succeed only in suppressing or masking sexual fears without eliminating them. The result is usually emotional superficiality and sexual licentiousness. The reduction and eventual elimination of sexual fear can be achieved only by rational insight, and, most of all, by the help of sexual partners who combine love with patience and trust.

fellatio Licking or sucking of the **penis**, which can lead to **orgasm.** Fellatio, like **cunnilingus**, is a common form of sexual activity. It is not a **perversion**. However, it is illegal, even between husband and wife, in most states. (See **sex legislation.**)

female (adjective and noun) Opposite of **male**. One of the two sexes, as determined by certain **sexual characteristics**. Also a person of female sex.

The biological dual concept of female and male has a parallel in the cultural dual concept of **femininity** and **masculinity**. However, unlike their biological counterparts, the terms "feminine" and "masculine" often imply certain cultural values which are open to question and subject to change. This ideological element in seemingly neutral terms has also affected the non-scientific use of the words "female" and "male." Nevertheless, it should be remembered that the individual character of human females or males is not so much determined by nature as by cultural influences.

femininity A quality of character or physical appearance considered to be typical of women.

In all human societies the biological difference between **female** and **male** is used as the basis for different social and **sexual roles**. Although such roles may vary from one time and culture to another, they are, in each case, declared to be "natural" and unchangeable. (See **masculinity.**)

63

In our own culture, femininity is usually equated with pretty looks, passivity, and sentimentality. As a result, the active social and sexual contributions of women are often underestimated or even denied. There is also a whole industry devoted to the cultivation of femininity by means of make-up, perfumes, hair-dyes, dresses, and jewelery. However, the proper use of such "feminine" accessories is meant to create nothing more than "sex appeal," a quiet attractiveness that leaves the sexual initiative to the male. In fact, there is a widespread mistaken belief that a woman's sexuality remains dormant unless awakened by the active approach of a man. This misconception is also the reason for the common tendency to picture a female as either a girl or a mother. A woman who is neither virgin nor wife can hardy avoid being considered as either a dangerous seductress or a dull person of no consequence. Women still have difficulties being accepted on equal terms as co-workers or colleagues. (See **patriarchy, woman.**)

feminism The attitude, philosophy, or social movement which demands equal rights for women.

feminist A person who fights for the **emancipation** of women in order to achieve the **equality of the sexes.**

fertility The ability to procreate.
More specifically: in men, fertility is the ability to cause **pregnancy** in a fertile woman; fertility in women is the ability to become pregnant by a fertile man.
Male and female fertility begins with **puberty** and comes to an end with the **climacteric.** (See also **infertility.**)

fetishist A man or a woman who is sexually more easily aroused by things (such as underwear, shoes, wigs) than by the person to whom they belong. Such a thing is then called a fetish. In some cases, a fetishist also becomes obsessed with certain parts of his partner's body, and thus the feet, **breasts,** or buttocks may become his fetish. When somebody is sexually excited only by inanimate objects or certain parts of the anatomy at the exclusion of a human partner, his behavior is called fetishism. It is a sexual **perversion.**

fetus Medical term for the unborn baby after the third month of **pregnancy.** (See also **embryo.**)

fidelity Specifically: marital fidelity. In our culture, where **monogamy** has become the only legitimate form of **marriage,** the partners are expected to restrict their sexual interest to one another. A husband or a wife who engages in **extramarital intercourse** commits **adultery,** which is usually considered sufficient ground for a **divorce.**

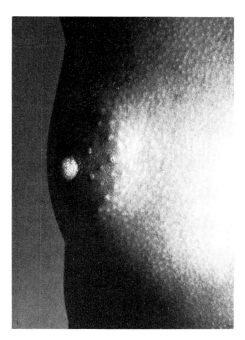

However, in most instances of marital infidelity, the marriage partners are less concerned with such legal considerations than with their personal disappointment. The marriage partner who has been "unfaithful" is often believed to have "betrayed" the marriage relationship, and the offended spouses tend to consider themselves forever deprived of the exclusivity to which they had felt entitled. Nevertheless, in such cases it can be useful to remember that no one is "unfaithful" as long as his marriage meets his needs for **love** and sexual **satisfaction.** Neither does adultery always have to destroy a marriage.

first love

A young person's first **love** is an overwhelming and incomparable experience. Boys and girls who are in love for the first time are blind to sobering circumstances and to the short-comings of their suddenly discovered sexual partners. The beloved seems perfect in every way, and capable of fulfilling the lover's most secret wishes, dreams, and desires.

However, this pleasant illusion rarely lasts very long. All human feelings change with time, and the first love is no exception. In some very rare cases, it leads to a more realistic permanent relationship. Most often, the spell just slowly wears off, and one's attention gradually turns to new partners. Occasionally, people continue to see each new acquaintance in the light of their early experiences. Such persons can easily become too critical. Others realize that their first love cannot be a model for all other relationships. Eventually, they may conclude that their former feelings were a childish expression of emotional immaturity.

Both of these attitudes seem unreasonable. The first love, by its very nature, is unsuited for comparisons. Nevertheless, there can be no doubt that it is an important event in everybody's life, and nobody is ever too young for it. (See also **crush.**)

first menstruation

A girl's first **menstruation** generally occurs between the ages of 11 and 13. It is a symptom of the beginning sexual maturation caused by **hormones,** which now continue to develop in the female body up to the time of the **menopause.**

Before her first menstruation, a young girl must be told that every woman experiences such monthly bleedings, that they are related to her ability to become pregnant, and that, in fact, they signalize the body's recurring preparation for a **conception.** At the same time, the girl has to be instructed in the proper genital hygiene. She should also be informed that, during menstruations, she might experience some slight physical discomfort, and that such symptoms need not indicate any illness.
All of these instructions, necessary as they are, cannot replace a proper **sex education.**

first sexual intercourse

Most boys and girls think, dream, and even talk about their first **sexual intercourse** long before it actually occurs. (Only very few emotionally disturbed people never think about sex.) All of these expectations,

hopes, fears, and fantasies can turn the eventual real experience into something of an anticlimax. Nevertheless, for all of us, the first sexual intercourse has a special meaning. These are some of its most important aspects:

- For the first time since infancy, we express love and affection without any restraint or emotional reservation.

- We commit ourselves to another human being and thus gain a new emotional distance from our parents.

- We have to come to terms with ourselves and our partner as to whether we should invite the chance of a pregnancy or use a method of **birth control.**

- If unmarried, we may risk a conflict with public morality, social **conventions,** religious commandments, or even the law. (See **premarital intercourse, sex legislation.**)

In the past, the first sexual intercourse was reserved for the **wedding night,** at least in the case of most women. (See **double standard.**) The young wife's **defloration** was her decisive sexual experience, as it had to prove both her own **virginity** and her husband's **virility.** The outcome of this crucial test could determine the entire future of a couple's marriage. Under these circumstances, the first sexual intercourse was often unduly dramatized and could turn into an excrutiating experience.

Today people are generally more relaxed in these matters, and the wedding night has lost most of its former exaggerated importance. Nevertheless, the first sexual intercourse can still create moments of tension and anxiety, as one or both of the sexual partners try to overcome their **modesty** and inexperience. In some cases, unfavorable external conditions, such as lack of time or privacy, can add to the emotional strain. Another source of frustration may be the fear of an **unwanted pregnancy** or worry about the correct application of birth-control methods. Certain sex partners may even resent or distrust each other. They may resort to sexual intercourse only because they have nothing to talk about. Others may just try to "prove something" to themselves because they fear being frigid or impotent.

Some girls or women are also afraid of possible bleeding or pain. However, the use of **tampons** and certain **petting** experiences already dilate the opening of the **vagina,** thus greatly facilitating the later insertion of a man's **penis.** Furthermore, with her mounting sexual **excitement** a woman reaches a point where her vagina opens spontaneously, thereby reducing the chance of pain. Finally, both sexual partners should know that pain during intercourse can be caused by a lack of lubrication. However, this lubrication is usually provided by the woman's own secretions. Only in exceptional cases is there any need for **lubricants.** In other words, although a woman may experience some slight discomfort during her first sexual intercourse, there is no need to fear any great pain. Men, on the other hand, who fear **impotence** or a **premature ejaculation,** should remember that such an occurrence on such an occasion would not disprove their sexual abilities. On the whole, people should not expect too much from their first sexual intercourse. Perfect sexual harmony or simultaneous orgasms of both partners are usually the result of time and practice.

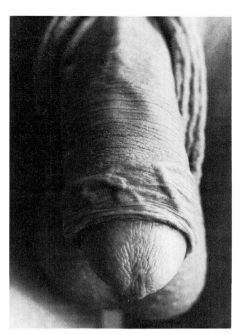

All of these observations point to the same truth: the first sexual intercourse can be no more than the beginning of a sexual relationship. It is just one step on the way to sexual and personal maturity.

In the future, the increasing **coeducation** of boys and girls at all age levels will help them to get to know each other well enough before they enter any sexual relationships. Thus sexual intercourse will follow, not precede, a personal understanding between the sexes.

flirt (From French "fleurette": amorous flattery) A psychological game in which one partner displays a certain erotic interest in the other who, in turn, responds with hints of approval or leaves his admirer deliberately in doubt.

Flirting is a pleasant form of erotic encounter, an intermediate stage between a polite acquaintance and a sexual relationship. Flirting is based on mutual attraction and keeps potential sexual partners in a pleasant state of suspense without allowing for intimacies. It is a playful way of indirect courtship without personal obligations.

foreplay A term used by certain people for the description of caresses that lead to **coitus.**

All gestures and physical movements that establish contact between sexual partners belong to the total experience of **sexual intercourse.** It is shortsighted to divide sexual activity into phases, acts, or chapters that have to build up to some sort of dramatic climax. Such a mechanistic view of sex can lead to severe misunderstandings and may ruin the chance for a truly intimate relationship. (See also **sex manual.**)

Sexual partners should never fear to break with prescribed behavioral patterns, but should rather explore their mutual desires, respond to each other's wishes, and follow their own instincts as the best method of achieving sexual **satisfaction.**

foreskin Moveable part of skin at the tip of the **penis,** usually covering the **glans.** In the case of an **erection,** the glans protrudes from the foreskin and becomes fully exposed.

In some very rare cases the foreskin proves too tight. Such a condition is called a **phimosis,** and it may require minor surgery. (See **circumcision.**) It is always necessary to wash the penis regularly, including the glans. In so doing, uncircumcised boys and men have to push back the foreskin, because residues of urine, perspiration, and some glandular secretions (smegma) may be trapped underneath.

fornication An old-fashioned term referring to **premarital** and **extramarital intercourse.**

As a legal term, it usually means sexual intercourse between unmarried partners. (See **sex legislation.**)

four-letter words

A euphemism for slang expressions referring to sexual or scatological matters. (See **Glossary of Sexual Slang** at end of volume.)

free love

A regular sexual relationship between a man and a woman without legalization by **marriage.**

In some cases, unmarried couples live together in the expectation of separating at some future date. Others do not get married because they object to the legal and moral implications of an official marriage. In still other cases, there are legal obstacles to getting married.

The institution of marriage is designed to reduce all other forms of cohabitation to a lower social status. Consequently, "free love" usually suffers from various legal, economic (taxes), and social disadvantages. For the same reason, in everyday language, the term "free love," which once had a positive, missionary quality, now generally carries overtones of disapproval and contempt.

French kiss

An open-mouth **kiss** which brings the tongues of both partners into direct contact.

The adjective "French" in this and other English terms for sexual objects or practices originally indicated disapproval and a tendency to characterize them as outlandish and abnormal. The French, who have always had a reputation for having a certain "savoir vivre," or, in other words, for being able to enjoy life to the full, were often credited with all those things that created feelings of guilt and embarrassment in other nations, although they were no less prevalent there than in France. Thus, at one time, a **venereal disease** was called "French disease" in England. (The French themselves called it "la maladie anglaise": the English disease.)

French letter

An old-fashioned euphemism for **condom.**

French postcards

See **dirty pictures.**

French tickler

Colloquial term for a **condom** with a rough or irregular surface, intended to increase vaginal stimulation.

friendship

Friendships help people to escape loneliness and to see themselves accepted on equal terms by others who share their opinions, concerns, or life-styles.

The fact that somebody has a friend proves his ability to establish personal contact. However, a lack of friends is not necessarily a symptom of failure or worthlessness, although it is an indication of how difficult close personal relationships can be, especially over a longer period of time. It is not always easy to find and keep a true friend. To a certain extent, it is also a matter of luck.

A person who has several close friends usually has a different relationship with each of them. On the other hand, there are also those friendships that arise out of a group experience such as in sports or in the army, where a feeling of togetherness and an all-embracing sense of companionship can blur the distinctions. Nevertheless, even within such groups there sometimes develop special relationships between two or more "buddies" who feel closer to each other than to the rest of their comrades.

Friendships between persons of different sex often have a character of their own. Sometimes girl-friends or boy-friends are chosen for reasons of prestige and popularity. At other times, such friendships become the basis for sexual relationships and even marriage. (See **dating**.)

A friendship can serve many purposes. Friends usually give each other a sense of being understood and appreciated. They help each other in their common endeavors, and stimulate each other's emotional and intellectual growth. A boy or a girl also needs a friend as a counterbalance to personal experiences with parents, older relatives, teachers, or other persons of authority. However, friendships are pleasant, useful, and, indeed, necessary at any age.

All friendships undergo changes in the course of time, and not all of them last. Sometimes it is better to be prepared for a separation than to cling to an empty or frustrating relationship. However, whenever a friendship comes to an end, there should be no ill feelings or accusations from either side. In the words of Oscar Wilde: "Laughter is not at all a bad beginning for a friendship, and it is far the best ending for one."

frigidity Inability of a woman to experience sexual pleasure or **orgasm.**

The causes of frigidity are mostly psychological. Even women who have a strong desire to love and to be loved can suffer from frigidity. However, whether a woman is frigid can be determined only by a professional diagnosis. In this case, professional treatment can usually bring the necessary help.

Sometimes unusual shyness, inexperience, and ignorance in sexual matters are mistaken for frigidity. In such cases, appropriate information and counselling can alleviate and, finally, eliminate the problem.

Frigidity and lack of orgasm in women do not mean **infertility.**

fun morality A popular modern term describing the ethics of **hedonism.** (See also **sexual ethics**.)

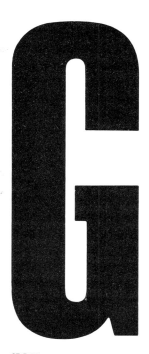

gay Slang for **homosexual.**

gay liberation A radical social movement devoted to the **emancipation** of **homosexuals.**

genital (adjective) Related to the **genitals.**

genital intercourse **Sexual intercourse** involving the **genitals** of both partners. More specifically: **coitus.**

genitals Sex organs. The organs which determine the sex of men and women, enable them to engage in sexual activity, and make procreation possible. There are external and internal genitals.

The **male** external genitals are: the **penis** and the **scrotum,** which contains the two **testicles.** Among the internal male genitals are the **spermatic ducts** and the prostate gland.

The **female** external genitals are called **vulva** and they consist of **labia majora, labia minora, clitoris,** and the vaginal opening. The internal female genitals are: the **vagina,** the **uterus,** the **Fallopian tubes,** and the **ovaries.**

The genitals serve several important functions:

- They influence the growth and health of the **body** by their production of **hormones.**

- When touched by a sexual partner, they can stimulate sexual **excitement.** (See **erogenous zones.**)

- They are instrumental in the **satisfaction** of the **sex drive.** (See **masturbation, petting, sexual intercourse.**)

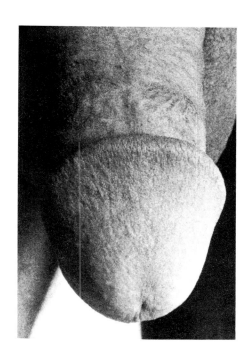

- Their anatomical form enables men and women to achieve a sexual union in **coitus.**
- They can serve the purpose of procreation. (See **conception, ovum, spermatozoa.**)

The close connection of the genitals with the excretive organs can hinder the development of a proper attitude towards both. Children experience their genitals first as excretive organs, and it is only later that they begin to understand the sexual functions of penis and vagina. Unfortunately, there sometimes develops a mental association between sex and excretion, which then manifests itself in the notion that sex is somehow "unclean" and "dirty." This notion can become the source of a serious **inhibition.**

It is one of the main tasks of **sex education** to provide children with a sensible attitude towards their genitals and human **sexuality** in general.

glans

Tip of the **penis.** The glans is usually thicker than the shaft of the penis. Being particuarly sensitive to the touch, the glans has a major function in the experience of sexual pleasure.

Both the **urethra** and the **spermatic duct** end in the glans.

go-go girl

A girl who dances professionally on a stage or elevated podium in bars or nightclubs, usually with exposed breasts ("topless") or even in complete nudity ("topless and bottomless"). The social functions of go-go dancing are similar to those of **strip-tease.** Some bars also feature "go-go boys."

golden wedding anniversary

The 50th wedding anniversary. The 25th is the "silver wedding anniversary," and the 60th is called "diamond wedding anniversary."

Until about a hundred years ago, a marriage lasting 25, 50, or more years was extremely rare. This was partly due to the fact that many women contracted fatal infections in childbed or died of exhaustion after too many births. It was therefore not unusual for a man to be widowed and remarried several times.

Today, because of the general increase in life expectancy, the average **marriage** lasts much longer than in the past. As a consequence, the meaning of marriage and of marital **fidelity** has also changed. The modern marriage usually outlasts the **family,** and, in addition, most women today survive their husbands. All of these changes make demands on the institution of marriage which were formerly unknown.

It has also become more obvious than ever that middle-aged and even aged men and women do have sexual interests and are capable of leading satisfying sexual lives. The capacity to remain sexually active depends more on expectations and attitudes than on biological age. Sexual relationships between older people have, of course, a character different from those between young or middle-aged men and women.

gonorrhea   The most common of the **venereal diseases.**

Gonorrhea is almost always contracted through **sexual intercourse** with an infected partner. It can also be transmitted through contaminated objects, such as towels, linens, or clothing, although this is extremely rare. The disease is caused by a bacterium called gonococcus, which usually first affects the **urethra** (in men), the **vagina** (in women), or the intestinal canal.

While many women who contract gonorrhea have no early noticeable symptoms, men experience a severe burning pain during urination about 3 to 9 days after infection. The orifice of the urethra at the tip of the **glans** is inflamed, and soon afterwards a yellowish discharge becomes apparent. (Such a discharge can also occur in infected females.)

If treated immediately, gonorrhea can easily be cured. However, if it remains untreated, it can spread inside of the body and result in serious complications, such as bladder inflammation, arthritis or irritation of the joints, and sterility. The baby of a mother who suffers from gonorrhea may also become infected during its **birth.** In order to prevent any possible eye-infections with gonococci, the eyes of newborn children are usually treated with a solution of silver nitrate. A person who has been cured of gonorrhea is not immune to a new infection.

group sex   Sexual intercourse between various partners within a group.

Such a group may be a **commune,** or a circle of married or single friends, or a so-called "swingers' club." Sometimes partners for group sex are solicited through newspaper ads. Participants meet at parties where they exchange their sexual partners or, as in the case of some nude parties, join the other guests in an **orgy.**

Group sex in one form or another has existed at all times, although today many people are much more open about it than their ancestors might have been in the past. Nevertheless, our society generally disapproves of the practice since it runs counter to the official demand for **monogamy.** On the other hand, sex in company with others and the exchange of sexual partners have always been part of the human sexual imagination as expressed in works of literature and art, or in the daydreams and fantasies of ordinary people. It is also true that in the course of history, not all cultures have demanded secrecy, privacy, or exclusiveness for sexual acts. In certain societies, group sex was and is an accepted fact of everyday life.

hair Hair style and length of hair are no indications of a person's character or sexual behavior. Certain hair styles or beards are related to religious traditions (orthodox Jews, Amish, Sikhs, and others). The fact that in most Western countries today women usually wear their hair longer than men is a matter of social convention. Such **conventions** vary from one time and place to another.

Women, because of the influence of female hormones, generally have softer and fuller hair. Baldness is practically restricted to men. Again, this is due to their hormonal structure and to hereditary factors. It is only in this sense that hair is a sexual characteristic.

During **puberty**, both boys and girls develop the growth of hair around the genitals (pubic hair) and under the armpits. Boys also begin to develop a beard and, usually, some hair on the chest. This hair has no particular function. It is, however, an obvious sign of sexual maturity. (See **sexual characteristics.**)

Some people are sexually stimulated by the sight of their partner's hair; others are indifferent or even disgusted by it. Some women, in fact, shave their legs and armpits in the belief that this will make them more attractive. Basically, such practices are a matter of taste.

hedonism (from the Greek "hedone": pleasure) A philosophy or a way of life based upon the belief that pleasure is the highest value.

Today the hedonistic attitude towards life in general and sex in particular is also known under the popular label "fun morality." Its proponents believe that sex is fun and, as such, needs no further justification. (See **sexual pleasure.**) "Fun morality" can therefore be described as a "morality of indulgence." However, such indulgence does not necessarily lead to licentiousness and irresponsibility. On the contrary, responsible hedonists try to avoid short-lived, dangerous, or destructive pleasures in favor of lasting personal satisfaction and the development and refinement of the best human potential. (See also **sexual ethics.**)

hermaphrodite

(After the Greek deities Hermes and Aphrodite) A person whose body combines male and female **sexual characteristics.**

In hermaphrodites, the **genitals** can be either underdeveloped, or their sexual identification can be in doubt. Sometimes both male and female genitals can be present. The cause of this malformation is usually a hormonal deficiency requiring medical treatment. Before treatment is possible, a determination of sex must be made.

heterosexual

(adjective and noun) From Greek "heteros": different, and Latin "sexus": sex. Literally translated, the term means that the sex drive is directed towards persons of a different sex. A heterosexual is a man who falls in love with women, or a woman who falls in love with men. Opposite of **homosexual.**

heterosexuality

is the term used for the heterosexual disposition leading to heterosexual behavior. It is the most common form of sexual orientation.

homosexual

(adjective and noun) From Greek "homos": same, and Latin "sexus": sex. Literally translated, the term means that the sex drive is directed towards persons of the same sex. A homosexual is a man who falls in love with other men, or a woman who falls in love with other women. Opposite of **heterosexual.** A homosexual woman is also sometimes called a **lesbian.**

homosexuality

is the term used for the homosexual disposition leading to homosexual behavior.

Homosexuality and heterosexuality are not clear-cut, separate, and irreconcilable entities, but rather matters of degree. Statistically speaking, the population as a whole displays a wide spectrum of sexual responses ranging from exclusive heterosexuality on one side to exclusive homosexuality on the other, with a large segment of **ambisexual** responses in between. Because of this many-shaded behavioral spectrum, it has proven difficult to provide commonly accepted, clear definitions of the terms "homosexual" and "homosexuality." It is much easier to recognize and define individual homosexual acts, and so to determine the extent of homosexual behavior.

Homosexual behavior (up to the point of orgasm) has been found to occur in 37% of the American male population. In many of these cases the homosexual experiences remain isolated incidents in an otherwise predominantly heterosexual life. However, it is certain that at least 4% of all men remain exclusively homosexual throughout their lives. For females the estimated incidence of homosexual behavior is about half that for males. (These figures are based on the findings by Kinsey et al. established in 1948 and 1953. There is some reason to believe that a new study today would result in higher percentages.)

Exclusive homosexuals have no more choice in their sexual orientation than exclusive heterosexuals have in theirs. Most of them become aware of their homosexuality after puberty. At the same time they realize that their sexual preference puts them at odds with their families, their friends, and society in general. The shock of this realization and the necessity to hide the most intense personal feelings can cause severe emotional problems. In some instances, professional treatment by a psychoanalyst can bring about a change to heterosexuality, if such a change is genuinely desired. In most cases, however, the treatment will be considered successful if it alleviates the patient's feelings of guilt and despair, and helps him to make a relatively successful adjustment to his homosexuality. This adjustment is difficult enough in any event, as the psychological problems of most homosexuals are caused less by their homosexuality than by society's reaction to it. This hostile reaction also contributes to the fact that deep and lasting relationships between homosexuals are rare. (See **promiscuity.**) Nevertheless, despite these difficulties, and although procreation between members of the same sex is not possible, homosexual relationships tend to be comparable to heterosexual relationships. They can express just as much tenderness, respect, responsibility, and love. Since the object of this love is the other person as a whole, homosexuality cannot be considered a **perversion.**

Traditionally, our Western Judeo-Christian culture has condemned homosexual acts as sinful, regardless of the circumstances. Only recently have some Christian churches reversed or modified their negative attitude (Quakers, Episcopalians, Methodists, United Church of Christ). Our increased scientific knowledge about human sexuality has also led some Lutheran and Roman Catholic theologians to re-examine the attitude of their churches and to free themselves of their former rigidity in this matter. There remains, however, a general uneasiness about the subject of homosexuality among most Christians.

Sometimes the claim is made that there is an increase of homosexuality today or that, in the past, such an increase caused the decline and fall of the Roman Empire or of some other great nation. These claims have no scientific value and cannot be supported by factual evidence. Statistical sex research has begun only recently. All available figures, therefore, are quite new. The lack of exact historical data rules out any comparison with the past. On the other hand, it is well known that the culture of ancient Greece, during its rise, and at its peak, included the open acceptance, indeed the encouragement, of homosexuality. It is also known that today such modern states as Sweden, Denmark, the Netherlands, Canada, Great Britain, France, Germany, and Japan tolerate homosexual behavior among their citizens without adverse effects on their national strength and economic efficiency. (See also **emancipation.**)

In the United States (except for Illinois and Connecticut), homosexual acts are illegal. Punishment ranges from a maximum of life imprisonment (in Georgia) to a minimum of a $100 fine (in Indiana). The American Law Institute in its Model Penal Code as well as the National Commission on Reform of Federal Criminal Laws have recommended that all sexual acts between consenting adults in private be legalized. (This would include homosexual acts.) However, public ignorance on the subject of homosexuality and public opposition to legal reform in this area are still extensive.

As long as this general attitude persists, homosexuality will create social and psychological problems for both homosexuals and heterosexuals. The situation was summarized by Sigmund Freud in a letter to an American mother: "Homosexuality is assuredly no advantage, but it is nothing to be ashamed of, no vice, no degradation, it cannot be classified as an illness. . . . It is a great injustice to persecute homosexuality as a crime, and cruelty too." Only better information and education of the American public will eventually give the American homosexual the same freedom from persecution and the same civil rights that he would enjoy as a citizen of most European, African, and Asian countries. (See also **aberration, masculinity, sex legislation, sexual roles, unnatural sex.**)

honeymoon

The period after the **wedding** when husband and wife begin to adjust to their new roles, and when they devote their full attention to each other.

During this delicate period of adjustment, many newly married couples take a honeymoon trip, in order to be undisturbed by their families and their friends. Such a honeymoon trip can also be considered a special vacation before settling down to the realities of everyday life.

For many couples today, the honeymoon no longer retains its former meaning and importance, as they often have had intimate personal contact with each other and, in some cases, already have lived together before the wedding for some time.

hooker

Slang term for a female **prostitute.**

hormones

Substances which are produced by the so-called endocrine glands and which are released into the bloodstream.

The normal physical development and health of the body depends on the proper functioning and balance of all hormonal glands.

The hormones produced by the sex glands (the **testicles** in men; the **ovaries** in women) are called sex hormones. They control the development of the **sexual characteristics,** male and female **fertility,** and the physiological and psychological reactions related to the **sex drive.** Although male and female hormones are present in both sexes, there is a considerable preponderance of male hormones (androgens) in men, and of female hormones (estrogens) in women.

husband

The male partner in a **marriage.**

hustler

A male **prostitute.** In most cases the term refers to **homosexual** prostitution. A hustler who engages in **heterosexual** prostitution is also sometimes called a **stud.**

hygiene The science of health. Preventive medicine. Also a euphemism for the cleaning of female **genitals,** the use of **tampons,** or special genital deodorants.

hymen A thin membrane stretched across and partly covering the opening of the **vagina.**

Since the hymen is usually ruptured during the **first sexual intercourse,** an intact hymen is often considered proof of a woman's **virginity.** (See **defloration.**) However, such proof is inconclusive, because the hymen may be torn not only during **coitus,** but also by **masturbation,** or as a consequence of certain athletic activities. In some cases, the hymen may even be absent.

The high value placed on a woman's intact hymen is a relic of former times, when women were the property of men. (See **double standard, man, patriarchy.**)

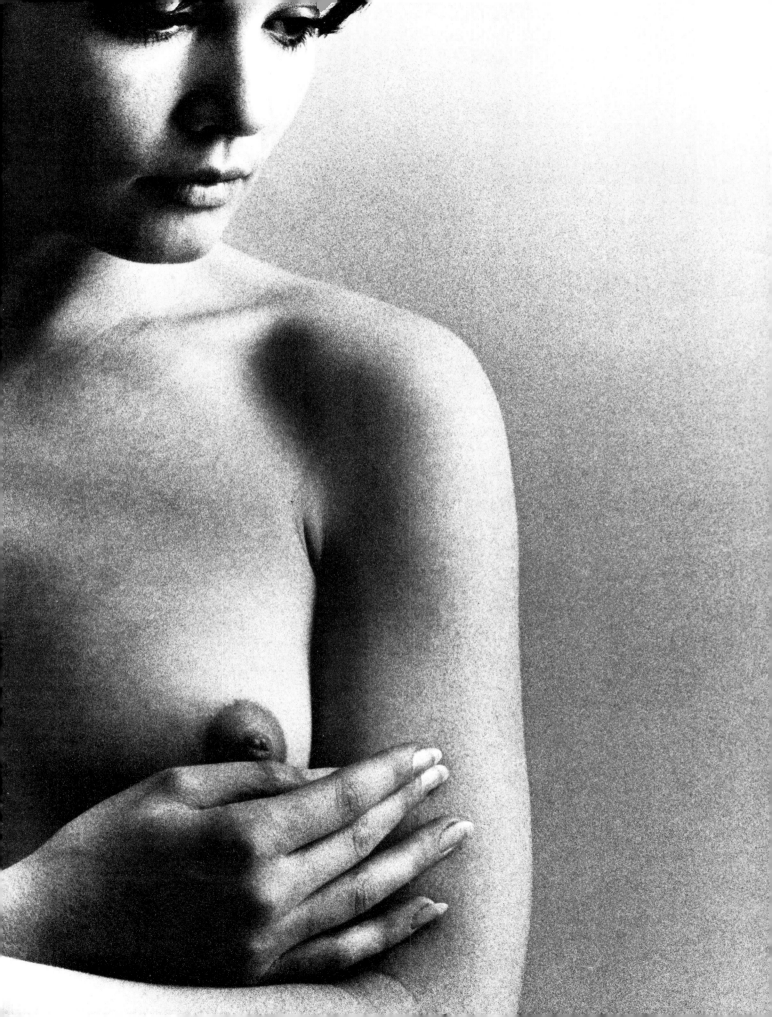

illegitimate child
The child of an unmarried mother.

The term "illegitimate" refers to the fact that, in our society, the conception and birth of children is socially approved and protected only within **marriage.** This means, in practical terms, that an illegitimate birth usually puts a child at a great disadvantage:

- The financial support provided by the father is often inadequate if not altogether absent.

- During the first three years of his life, a child needs the constant presence and care of his mother. However, many unwed mothers have to work in order to support themselves. As a consequence, their children may not receive the necessary attention.

- In later years, illegitimate children can encounter prejudice and social discrimination.

Some of these difficulties are compounded in the case of children who have to grow up without help from either parent and who remain unadopted.
The fight against such problems demands various medical, social, legal, and educational measures. (See **birth control, double standard, emancipation, extended family, premarital intercourse, sex education, unwanted pregnancy.**)

impotence
Sexual disorder in the male: inability to have sexual intercourse, due to the lack of an **erection** of the penis.

Chronic impotence in men who otherwise experience erections and ejaculations almost always has psychological causes, which can only be discovered and eliminated by professional treatment. An occasional inability to have an erection should not be considered impotence. It can usually be attributed to some unfavorable factors in a particular situation. In medical language the term "impotence" covers a wide variety of sexual and procreational impediments in men and women.

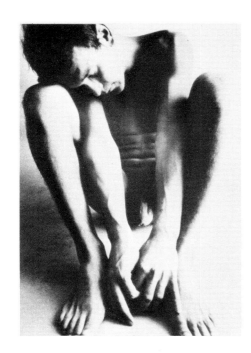

incest

Sexual intercourse between close relatives, such as parent and child, or brother and sister.

Incestuous relationships are illegal in the United States and in most other countries. (See **sex legislation.**) The reason normally given is that children born as a result of such relationships might, to an unproportionate extent, be afflicted with hereditary diseases.

The incest **taboo** is one of the oldest taboos of mankind, and its violation has almost universally carried severe penalties. Exceptions have been extremely rare. One example is ancient Egypt, where the pharaoh was compelled by law to marry his sister. This practice continued over many centuries without apparent negative consequences up to the days of Cleopatra, who was married to her brother Ptolemy.

infertility

(or sterility) The inability to procreate.

A couple's inability to achieve a pregnancy can result from male or female infertility.

A man's infertility may be caused by **impotence, castration,** or **sterilization,** or it may be due to a lack of fertile sperm cells in his semen. (See **ejaculation.**) A woman's infertility, if not also caused by castration or sterilization, can result from a malfunction of her **ovaries,** or from the after-effects of certain diseases, such as tuberculosis or **gonorrhea.** Apart from such obvious causes for infertility, there may be a variety of others that are more subtle and complicated. Sometimes the cause cannot be determined.

In some very rare cases, a couple remains childless simply because they never have sexual intercourse during the woman's fertile period. (See also **rhythm method.**)

infidelity See **fidelity.**

inhibition

Specifically: sexual inhibition. An unconscious checking or restraining of those impulses that are caused by the **sex drive.**

Inhibitions are the result of social conditioning, training, and education. To a certain extent, they are necessary for an orderly functioning of society, for example as caution, courtesy, tactfulness, and **modesty.** (See also **conventions.**)

However, if sexual inhibitions become too strong, they can cripple a person's **sexual development** and prevent him from achieving emotional **maturity.** (See also **prudery.**)

Sexual inhibitions can manifest themselves in sexual **fear,** aversion to unfamiliar sexual practices, disgust with one's own sex or hate of the opposite sex, an underdeveloped or exaggerated interest in sexual matters, or generally, in an inability to **love.**

Inhibitions are cause for serious concern only when they impair relationships with other people and cannot be overcome by sincere conscious effort. There are also unrecognized sexual inhibitions which may manifest themselves indirectly in depressive moods, emotional instability, or even physical ailments. People who suspect sexual inhibitions to be the source of their personal problems or who know that they do, in fact, suffer from serious sexual inhibitions, should seek professional help.

inversion From Latin "inversio": turning around (i.e., of the sex drive). A term sometimes used for **homosexuality.** According to the same terminology, a homosexual is called an invert.

I.U.D. Intra-uterine (contraceptive) device.

The intra-uterine device is an old method of **birth control** already known to the ancient Greeks and Persians. In recent decades, new types of such devices have been developed, and they are now in use in many parts of the world. The best known of these devices is perhaps the "loop," although the "shield," the "spring," and the "bow" are also popular.

As the name indicates, the I.U.D. is inserted by a doctor into the **uterus,** where it prevents pregnancy. At the present time, there is still no satisfactory explanation of how the device works. It is known, however, that it is almost 100% effective.

Despite its obvious virtues, this birth-control method has several disadvantages. For example, the device can in some cases be expelled from the uterus, or it can slip out without the woman's knowledge. There is also a possibility of infection, or of bleeding and pain, which may demand the removal of the device.

jealousy

A jealous person fears that his sexual partner might lose interest in him and turn his attention to other people or other matters.

A certain amount of jealousy can be an expression of love and true concern. However, it can also be a symptom of low self-esteem or egotism. In these cases, jealousy can easily become an obsession, destroying every possibility for an intimate, personal relationship.

How far jealousy is justified in a specific case depends very much on individual standards. People who feel that they are unusually jealous, and who, by their attitude, cause misery in others or themselves, should seek professional counselling.

jus primae noctis

(Latin: the right of the first night) Until well into the 18th century, the feudal lords in certain parts of Europe claimed the right to deflower the brides of their serfs. (See **defloration.**)

Today this custom may appear strange and even unbelievable. However, most opera-lovers are probably aware of its existence, as it serves as a starting point for the plot of Mozart's opera "The Marriage of Figaro." (The enlightened Count Almaviva has publicly renounced his "right of the first night," but regrets having done so when he falls in love with the bride of his servant Figaro.)

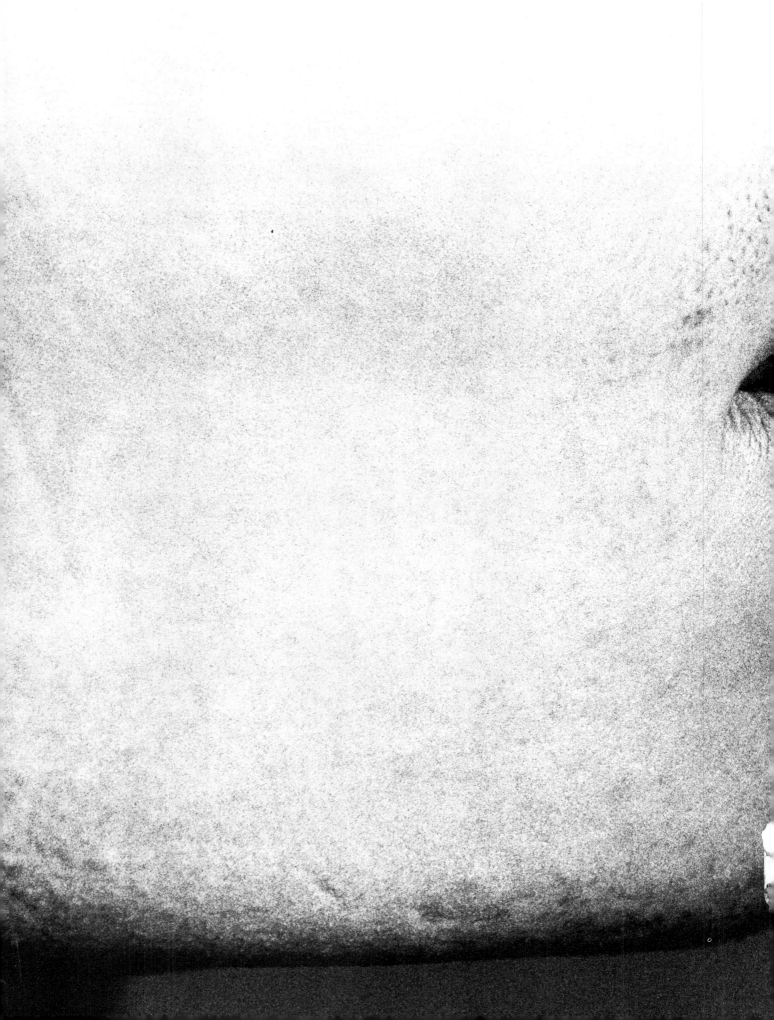

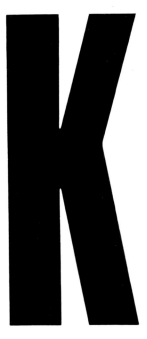

kiss Touching or caressing with the lips.
In our Western culture, kissing has always been a very personal expression of respect, **friendship,** or **love.**
In certain other cultures, people rub their noses against each other, a custom that probably has its roots in the animalistic instinct to "smell each other out."

Parents kiss children, men kiss a woman's hand, people respectfully kiss the ring of a bishop, a French general kisses his soldiers as he decorates them with medals, married and unmarried couples express their love for each other with tender or passionate kisses—in short, there are innumerable reasons and occasions for kissing which depend on various social **conventions.**

A kiss between sexual partners can have many different meanings, depending on the circumstances and on their individual feelings. There is a wide spectrum of kisses ranging from the slight touching of the lips to the passionate open-mouth kiss, involving the tongues of both partners (**French kiss**).

The mouth is one of the **erogenous zones,** and the touch of the lips and the tongue provides a very intense and intimate contact which can stimulate and increase sexual **excitement** to the point of **ecstasy.** Our feelings during a kiss, whether consciously controlled (see **necking**) or freely expressed, prove the close interdependence of our emotional and physical reactions.

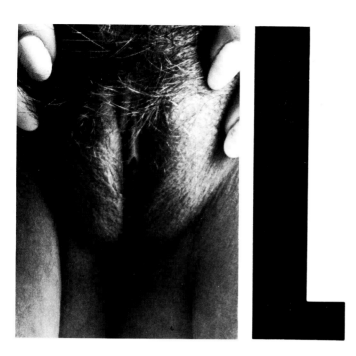

L

labia majora (Latin: "the greater lips") The outer lips of the **vulva.** During **puberty, hair** (the so-called "pubic hair") begins to grow on the labia majora.

labia minora (Latin: "the smaller lips") The inner lips of the **vulva,** which lie between the **labia majora.**

lesbian (adjective and noun) A term sometimes used for a **homosexual** woman and her sexual behavior. In ancient Greece, the island of Lesbos was known as the home of the poetess Sappho, who wrote many love poems in praise of her girl students.

lesbianism A term sometimes used for female **homosexuality.**

libido A psychoanalytic term referring to the fundamental psychic energy whose dynamic expression is **love.**
A person's libido comprises not only his love for a sexual partner, but also that for himself, his parents, children, friends, or humanity in general.
In early **childhood,** the libido is directed towards the child's own self. (See **narcissism.**) Later, parts of the libido are gradually transferred to the parents (see **Oedipus complex**) and then also to other persons, objects, and ideas. (See also **sublimation.**)

loop An intra-uterine contraceptive device. (See **I.U.D.**)

love Different people may associate the word "love" with different things, such as **friendship, desire, tenderness, passion,** or **sexual intercourse.** All of these terms refer to contacts and relationships that correspond to fundamental human needs.

The need to be close to someone may be described as a natural expression of human **sexuality.** However, it has to be remembered that sexual needs can appear in many shapes and forms, and that they may be satisfied in just as many ways. It is for this reason that every analysis or description of love must remain unsatisfactory. Only one thing is certain: a person who is all to himself, without anyone to love, cannot lead a truly human life.

Today every kind of sexual attraction between people is called love, and there is a general assumption that it should lead not only to sexual intercourse, but also to **marriage.** However, this concept of love is relatively new. Until well into the 19th century, love was not usually considered a precondition of marriage. The prosperity and continuity of the then **extended family** were believed to be more important than the mutual satisfaction of two people. The complete sexual compatibility of husband and wife was not seen as decisive, and was generally not expected.

The Greek and Roman idea of love was even more different from our modern concept. In ancient times, people put the emotional emphasis on the **sex drive** itself, not on its object. Love, for them, was a driving force that originated in the lover. It was directed towards others, but its strength was not dependent on their reactions. Someone was loved, not because he was desirable in himself, but because the love felt for him made him appear desirable. This view was summarized in the Greek saying: "The god of love dwells in the lover, not in the beloved." It was always the god of love who was worshipped, never another person. Love could be frustrated, if it remained unaccepted, but it could not be disappointed. There was no such thing as the modern "unhappy love."

In contrast to this philosophy, love today is most often seen as an attracting force which originates in the beloved and attracts the lover. The beauty or excellence of the beloved is the cause of love and its only justification. As a consequence, people are usually preoccupied not with the love they themselves feel, but with the object of their love. This love-object, the other person, is therefore often idealized to a point where eventual disappointment becomes inevitable. In other words, men and women are more concerned with receiving love than with giving it, and they tend to expect, indeed even demand, too much from each other.

The disadvantages resulting from this modern understanding of love can, perhaps, be avoided, if we return to an examination of our fundamental needs as human beings. Sexual love alone cannot satisfy all our needs for human contact. Love is more than sexual desire. This realization is best expressed in the Christian concept of **agape,** a selfless, tolerant love for our fellow men, who share with us our shortcomings and imperfections. Such an attitude is also the best foundation for a happy sexual relationship. (See also **romance.**)

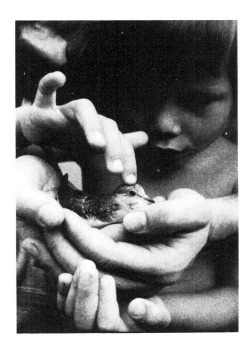

As this brief summary indicates, love is subject to various social and historical influences. Our modern concept of love is the result of a long and complicated cultural development, and it may well continue to change in the future. No predictions are possible, but this much can already be learned: for our own love-relationships, we should not simply follow established patterns, or models presented by movies, records, or television. Instead, we should try to develop truly personal contacts with those we love.

love potion   See **aphrodisiac.**

lubricants

There are substances which facilitate the insertion of the **penis** into the **vagina.** Sexual **foreplay** usually stimulates vaginal secretion which adequately prepares the female body for **coitus.** If the vagina does not provide a sufficient amount of secretion, the insertion of the penis can be painful. In such cases the application of a lubricant is advisable. It is also necessary for **anal intercourse.**

The most simple lubricant is saliva, but there are also a number of special lubricants on the market, of which Vaseline and KY are perhaps the most commonly known. Some **condoms** are prelubricated by the manufacturer.

lues   See **syphilis.**

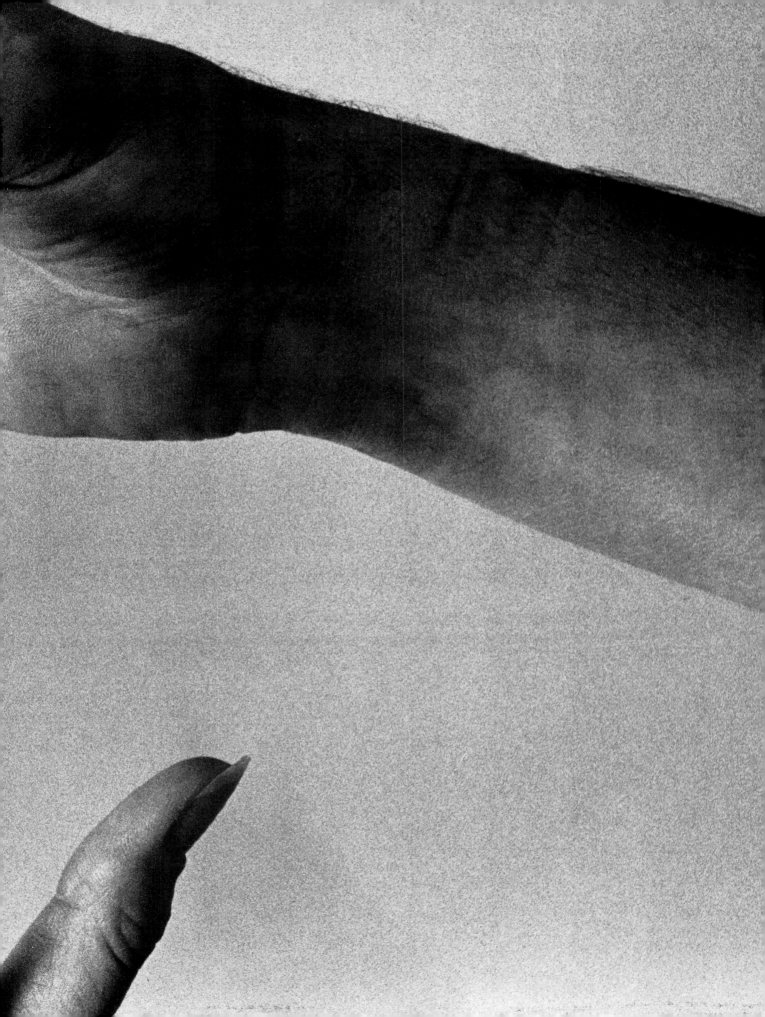

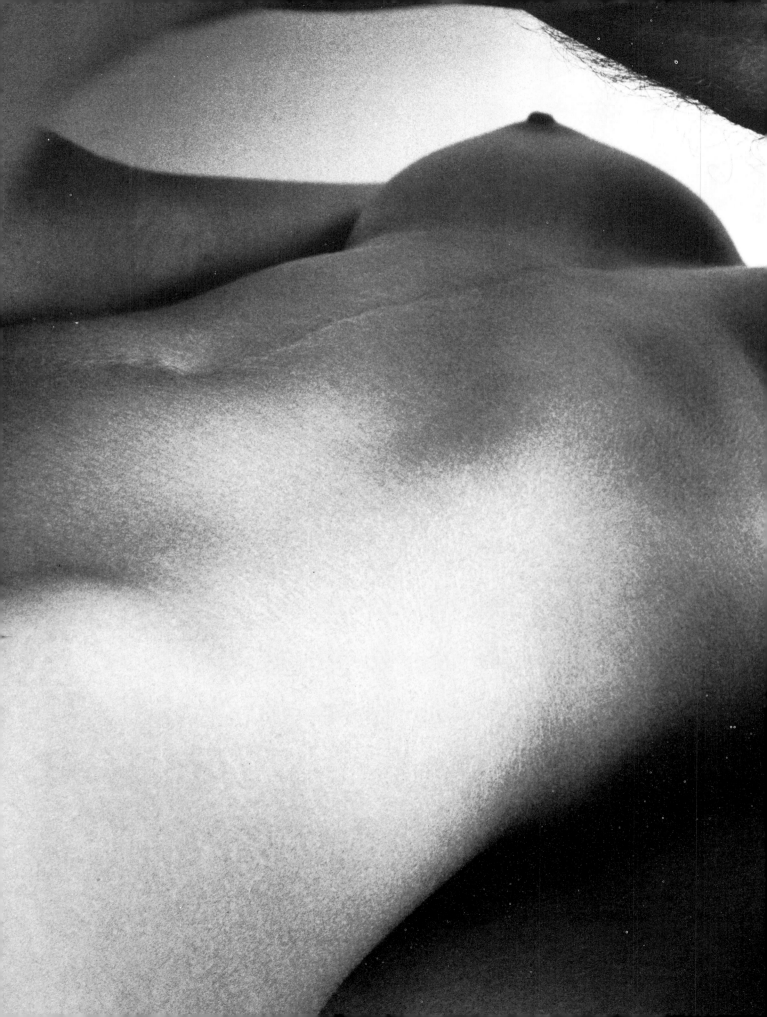

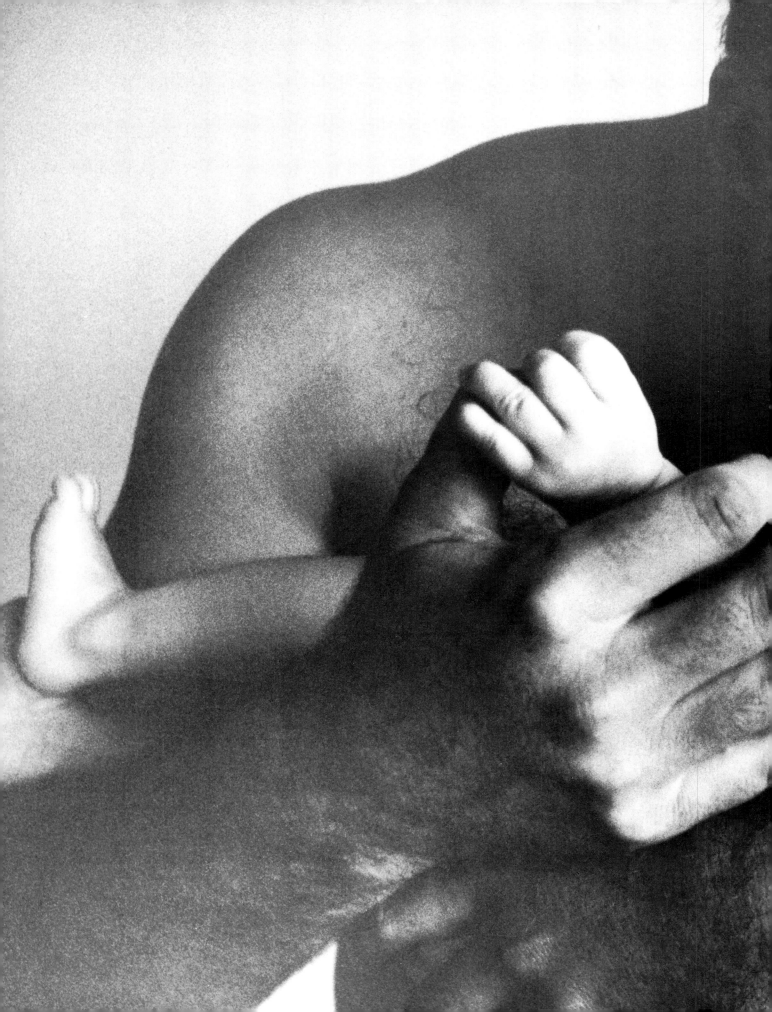

machismo A Spanish term referring to a particular brand of **masculinity** which manifests itself in fanatical sexual pride, **jealousy,** and an exaggerated concern with sexual **potency.**
Machismo is an extreme expression of **male supremacy.** (See also **double standard, patriarchy.**)

male (adjective and noun) Opposite of **female.** One of the two sexes, as determined by certain **sexual characteristics.** Also a person of male sex.
The biological dual concept of male and female has a parallel in the cultural dual concept of **masculinity** and **femininity.** However, unlike their biological counterparts, the terms "masculine" and "feminine" often imply certain cultural values which are open to question and subject to change. This ideological element in seemingly neutral terms has also affected the non-scientific use of the words "male" and "female." Nevertheless, it should be remembered that the individual character of human males or females is not so much determined by nature as by cultural influences.

male chauvinism A term intended to describe the attitude of men who claim privileges because of their sex. (See **double standard, patriarchy.**)
The word "chauvinism" (after a French super-patriot by the name of Chauvin) is usually employed to characterize an exaggerated and fanatic patriotism.

male supremacy A polemical term referring to the fact that in most societies men dominate women. (See **patriarchy.**) In modern times this state of affairs has increasingly come under attack by women and men devoted to sexual liberation and **emancipation.**

man An adult human **male.** Also a collective term meaning "human being(s)," and referring to both men and women.

The biological differences between men and women have always been used as a basis for different social roles. Throughout history, men have usually been socially dominant as hunters, warriors, producers, priests, and heads of their families.

At the same time, women were relegated to a lower social status. (See **patriarchy, woman.**) These social roles were, of course, also reflected in the concepts of **masculinity** and **femininity.** However, it seems that these concepts are now beginning to change, as the **emancipation** of women leads to a greater **equality of the sexes.** In the future, men may lose their dominant social position, but they may very well profit in other respects, as the "battle of the sexes" is gradually replaced by increasing cooperation. (See also **sexual roles.**)

marriage The closest permanent relationship between one woman and one man, resulting from a mutual agreement of both, which is publicly declared and officially recognized. (See also **monogamy.**)

The marriage contract regulates the legal aspects of property rights, parental control, inheritance, and other such matters, and remains effective until terminated by the death of one or both partners, or by **divorce.** The legal privileges extended to married couples are aimed at strengthening marriage as an institution and at discouraging other social arrangements, such as **free love.**

Apart from such official aspects, marriage can be seen as a private decision by two people to enter a permanent sexual relationship. It could even be argued that, emotionally, every long-term sexual relationship has the character of a marriage, regardless of its official status. However, the absence of public recognition can put a strain on such relationships which is unknown to legally married couples. The proper evaluation of marriage requires, therefore, a study of all its psychological, social, religious, legal, and economic aspects. It is on this basis alone that an individual can make a valid decision as to whether he should get married or not. (See **single.**)

The fact that two people get married does not necessarily mean that they also found a **family.** But even if they do, the life of this family is often not more than an episode within the marriage. Statistically speaking, marriages today last almost twice as long as they did a hundred years ago. (See **golden wedding anniversary.**) These changes in the concept of marriage reflect the greater social and technological changes that have taken place in the recent past. It is entirely possible that the meaning, and even the form, of marriage will change even more drastically in the future.

marriage counsellor A professionally trained person, usually a psychologist, social worker, minister, or physician, who offers proper education and advice on sexual and psychological problems to married couples and to young people who are planning to marry.

Marriage counselling is closely related to **sex education,** and it may be offered to individuals as well as to couples and groups of couples. Some colleges offer courses in marital education.

Whenever marital difficulties arise today, professional counselling, which is based on scientific research, is preferable to the advice of relatives or friends. (See **family.**)

marriage manual   See **sex manual.**

masculinity
A quality of character or physical appearance considered to be typical of men.

In all human societies the biological difference between **male** and **female** is used as the basis for different social and **sexual roles.** (See also **man, woman.**) Such roles may vary from one time and culture to another. Nevertheless, in order to insure their acceptance, each society presents them as "natural" and unchangeable. Failure to conform to these roles is therefore usually punished not just as a breach of custom, but as a deviation from "nature."

In our own culture, masculinity is generally believed to manifest itself in rugged looks and extrovert, active, and aggressive behavior. In contrast, a smooth, sensuous physique and a quiet, introvert, passive demeanor are usually associated with **femininity.**

These cultural stereotypes are imprinted early on children's minds, for instance when they are told that boys are made of "snips and snails and puppy dog tails" and girls of "sugar and spice and everything nice."

Later, in adult society, women are supposed to be sensitive, receptive, and dominated by feelings, while men are considered to be demanding, productive, and largely controlled by reason. In short, our concepts of masculinity and femininity mirror the values of a society in which men dominate and women serve. (See **patriarchy.**)

It is obvious that not every man and every woman can hope to live up to these concepts. In many cases the sexual roles prove to be too confining. However, people who try to break out of them can encounter considerable difficulties, particularly if they themselves remain confused about their social and sexual identities. This confusion is the result of a life-long ideological indoctrination that constantly misrepresents cultural values as biological facts. (See **unnatural sex.**)

Thus a man who begins by doubting his own masculinity may end up doubting his maleness. Finding himself considered a "sissy" by others, he may wrongly conclude that he is a man only by mistake, and that he should rather be a woman or, at least, dress and behave like one. (See **transsexualism, transvestite.**) Others may, for the same reason, develop a fear of **impotence** and a constant need to "prove their masculinity" by turning into promiscuous brutes. (See **Don Juan, machismo.**) Still others believe that a lack of masculinity is identical with **homosexuality.** In actual fact, however, homosexuality and masculinity (or the lack of it) are no more related than homosexuality and left-handedness. There are too many effeminate heterosexuals and too many super-masculine homosexuals to justify such a simplistic jump to conclusions.

masochism

Need to be hurt or experience pain in order to find sexual satisfaction. A sexual **perversion.**

masochist

A person who enjoys being humiliated, hurt, or abused.

masturbation

Sexual self-stimulation, manipulation of **genitals** leading to **orgasm.**

Although it is not unusual for sexual partners to masturbate each other (mutual masturbation), masturbation occurs most freqently as "solitary sex" without partners. It is the simplest and most common form of sexual activity, always available, and known to both sexes in all age groups.

Children may play with their genitals as they begin to explore their bodies. Discovering some pleasurable feeling, they may seek to repeat the experience and thus, all by themselves, learn to masturbate. Young people, particularly after puberty, masturbate often because they do not have the opportunity for sexual intercourse.

For **single** adults, masturbation is also often the only way to find sexual satisfaction. Even married men and women may, on occasion, resort to masturbation during periods of separation, or when one marriage partner is sick or unavailable for other reasons.

Finally, masturbation is also practiced by people who are lonely, or who cannot find suitable partners because of old age.

It is hard to understand today how such a universal and harmless practice as masturbation could ever have been universally condemned. Nevertheless, this was the case in most Western countries until a few decades ago.

Ignorant doctors, in the name of science, advanced the most fantastic and nonsensical theories as to the dangers of masturbation, claiming, among other things, that it led to acne, tuberculosis, or even insanity. In spite of the fact that absolutely no evidence for such claims was ever presented, these superstitions were widely believed and can, in fact, occasionally still be encountered today.

The fact of the matter is, however, that masturbation does neither physical nor mental harm. Nor is there such a thing as "excessive" masturbation. The frequency of possible orgasms (whether through masturbation or other forms of sexual activity) varies considerably from one individual to the next. There is no "right" amount of sex that can serve as a standard for everybody. There is also no way in which any outsider can tell whether a boy or girl, a man or a woman, privately masturbates or not.

matriarchy

A form of society in which all important decisions are made by women.

In the past, certain cultures were dominated by women. However, in the course of history, these matriarchal societies have been replaced by male-dominated cultures. (See **patriarchy.**)

113

maturity   The state of being fully developed.

In human beings, the process of maturation is rather lengthy, and influenced by a variety of factors such as climate, quality of nutrition, and degree of civilization. In our own culture, people normally reach their physical maturity much earlier than their mental and emotional maturity. (See **puberty.**) However, because of a general **acceleration** of physical growth among today's teenagers, it is advisable to judge each young person individually in this respect. For example, there is no iron rule that could help us decide once and for all when someone is mature enough to begin a sexual relationship, or to marry, or to become a parent.

Obviously, maturity is not simply a matter of years. However, a concrete definition of maturity is extremely difficult. We might, perhaps, call a person mature who has learned to live with the inevitable discrepancy between his aspirations and his achievements, and whose attitude towards reality is equally free from resentment and resignation.

Very often, the word "maturity" is also used as a relative term, meaning an attitude or a kind of behavior that is "appropriate" for a certain age or social position. According to this usage, even a teenger who is still growing can be considered mature if he behaves in the way that is expected of him. However, this approach to the problem of maturity is not without drawbacks. For example, how can one decide which kind of sexual behavior should be considered "mature" for a teenager? As long as sexual intercourse is restricted to married adults, the suspicion remains that many young people who are described as mature by their elders are merely over-adjusted and have, in fact, repressed their sexual needs and desires.

member   The term "male member" (Latin: "membrum virile") is occasionally used in reference to the **penis.**

ménage à trois   (French: "household of three") A steady sexual relationship (resembling a marriage) between three partners, of whom two may be legally married to each other.

A "ménage à trois" usually consists of one man and two women, occasionally of one woman and two men. Since this kind of private arrangement can be interpreted as a sort of unofficial **bigamy,** it is considered immoral by most people. The lack of social approval together with the possible conflicts between the partners themselves put a particular strain on such relationships, and very few of them last long.

menarche   Medical term for the **first menstruation.**

menopause   The time in a woman's life when her menstrual bleeding begins to recur less frequently until it finally ceases altogether (usually between the ages of 45 to 50).

The menopause ends the woman's ability to conceive and can also produce other physical and psychological changes. However, these changes do not affect her **sex drive** and her sexual capacities, which remain undiminished. (See also **golden wedding anniversary.**)

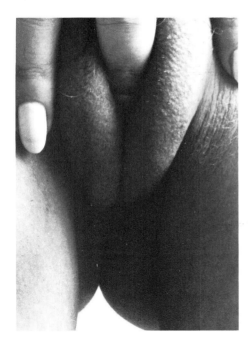

menstrual cycle

The biological process which takes place in the female body between two menstruations.

The cycle begins on the first day of a menstruation and ends on the day before the next menstruation. The length of menstrual cycles (measured in numbers of days) is subject to variation. (See also **rhythm method.**)

menstruation

(sometimes also called "period") A periodic discharge of blood and other materials from the reproductive organs of a sexually mature female. A menstruation may be accompanied by some physical discomfort, although many women experience hardly any inconvenience at all.

In most women, menstruation recurs about every 4 weeks (28 days). The time beginning with the first day of a menstruation and ending with the day before the next menstruation is called the **menstrual cycle.** The length of menstrual cycles as well as the duration of individual menstruations are subject to variation. Usually, each menstruation or period lasts between 2 to 5 days. During this time, women wear sanitary napkins or **tampons** which absorb the menstrual flow and thus allow for a continuation of normal daily activities. The **first menstruation** (or **menarche**) of a girl occurs when she reaches **puberty,** usually between the ages of 11 to 13. However, neither an early nor a late arrival of the menarche is cause for alarm. A woman's menstruations cease during her 5th decade. (See **climacteric, menopause.**)

Some women feel increased sexual desire before or during their menstruations. Nevertheless, many men and women avoid sexual intercourse during that time for esthetic and other reasons. However, there is no need to make this a universal rule. (See **sexual intercourse during menstruation.**)

During a pregnancy, menstruation ceases. However, the absence of an expected menstruation is not necessarily a **symptom of pregnancy.** On the other hand, it is not impossible that bleeding can occur even after a **conception** without terminating the pregnancy. In these and similar cases, where suspicious or unusual irregularities occur, a physician should be consulted.

minor

A person who is under age, that is, less than 21 years old.

Minors are subject to a number of legal restrictions not imposed on adults (legal adulthood or majority begins with the twenty-second year). Minors usually are subject to parental control, and are not allowed to buy liquor, hold certain jobs, or serve on juries. If they find themselves in trouble with the law, they also receive special consideration at the hands of law-enforcement officials, since they are generally treated as either "juvenile delinquents" (under 18 years in most states) or "youthful offenders" (over 18). However, the exact age limits for these and similar legal distinctions vary from state to state. For example:

- The minimum age for **marriage** without parents' consent ranges from 17 (males) and 18 (females) in Georgia to 21 (both sexes) in Kentucky, Mississippi, Montana, Ohio, Pennsylvania, Rhode Island, South Dakota, Vermont, Virginia, West Virginia, and Wyoming. In the other states the respective minimum ages lie between these extremes, with the female minimum age usually lower than that required for males.

- The minimum age for marriage with parents' consent ranges from 0 in Mississippi (for both sexes) to 18 in Florida and Michigan (also for both sexes). In the other states, the minimum ages lie between these extremes, with the female minimum age usually lower than that required for males.

- The age of consent to **sexual intercourse** ranges from 7 in Delaware and 12 in Louisiana and Tennessee to 18 in Arizona, California, Colorado, Florida, Idaho, Kansas, Kentucky, Massachusetts, Minnesota, Mississippi, Montana, Nebraska, New York, North Dakota, South Dakota, Texas, Utah, Washington, Wisconsin, and Wyoming. In all other states, the age of consent lies somewhere between these extremes, the age of 16 being the most commonly listed. Sexual intercourse with a girl under the age of consent is punishable as **statutory rape.**

Undoubtedly, the lack of conformity in these and similar laws in various states can lead to undesirable consequences. The 1970 Supreme Court decision to grant the right to vote in Federal elections to 18-year-olds is perhaps indicative of a certain public trend to reconsider the issue of legal rights for minors. (See also **acceleration, emancipation, maturity.**)

miscarriage

Spontaneous premature end of an advanced **pregnancy** resulting in death of **fetus.** A termination of pregnancy can also be purposely induced. (See **abortion.**) A miscarriage after the 24th week of pregnancy is called a stillbirth.

miscegenation   Mixing of the races.

In the United States, the term is usually applied to interracial marriages between whites and blacks. Several Southern states have so-called "miscegenation laws," which make such marriages illegal. However, according to a recent Supreme Court decision, these laws must now be considered unconstitutional.

modesty

A sense of reserve, discretion, or embarrassment in regard to genitals or excretive organs and their functions.

Modesty is the result of conscious and unconscious educational influences. Such influences suggest that certain things in the physical and emotional spheres be protected or hidden from others. The extent to which such influences make themselves felt depends on the attitudes and **conventions** of any given society.

The sense of modesty is usually less prominent towards familiar sexual partners, intimate friends or relatives, or towards a physician. However, normal modesty can increase to the point of bashfulness and uneasiness towards persons of the opposite sex. On the other hand, it can often be reduced or even eliminated by the use of **drugs,** such as alcohol.

A small child has no sense of modesty whatsoever. On the contrary, he shows a strong interest in excrement, and openly enjoys nudity and the sight and touch of his own and other people's genitals. (See **childhood.**)

For an adult, a moderate amount of modesty facilitates his adjustment to the social conventions of his time. In adults, a total lack of modesty as well as its exaggeration are symptoms of an emotional disorder. (See **prudery.**)

monogamy

Marriage of one man to one woman. Opposite of **polygamy.**

Monogamy has become the only accepted form of marriage in most parts of the world. For the duration of a monogamous marriage, either spouse is legally prevented from marrying a second or third partner. Of course, the possibility of **divorce** and remarriage can, in some cases, lead to something like "successive polygamy," meaning that one person can still, in the course of his life, be married to several partners.

The strict demand for monogamy as the only legitimate outlet for sexual expression cannot satisfy all human sexual needs. This is evident from the fact that society finds itself confronted with various social and sexual phenomena which, although well known, are commonly rejected, suppressed, denied, or barely tolerated, such as **premarital intercourse, free love, prostitution,** certain **perversions, strip-tease, pornography,** and other forms of **obscene** material or behavior. All of these things result from the repression of sexual wishes, which try to find some sort of gratification, however incomplete it might be. To a certain extent, such repression is unavoidable and can be considered the necessary price that society has to pay for the proven advantages of monogamy. Nevertheless, there is no need to become dogmatic about it. The fact that, so far, monogamy is the best available option does not mean it has to become the only one. It is therefore very well possible to support monogamy as a social institution while realizing at the same time that it should not, indeed cannot, be imposed on everyone. There is also no compelling reason why all **single** people should always practice total sexual **abstinence.** In fact, the institution of monogamy can only gain in dignity by the abandonment of bigotry and hypocrisy and the adoption of a more rational attitude in such matters.

Occasionally, one can hear the opinion that men are naturally polygamous, while women are said to be destined for monogamy. According to this view, women want and need only one man to whom they can devote their entire lives. Men, on the other hand, are believed to need several women before and outside of marriage. Such arguments cannot but lead to a sexual **double standard,** which extends to men sexual privileges denied to women.
In order to avoid the charge of **sexism,** certain other people claim that all human beings are naturally polygamous, and that a monogamous life dulls, indeed kills, their sexual drives. However, it is also unlikely that a life of sexual **promiscuity** can offer complete emotional satisfaction, since sex is the vehicle for deeper human needs, and the human contact provided by indiscriminate encounters remains too superficial.

A realistic evaluation of monogamy and its alternatives will have to admit that a life-long sexual relationship with only one partner cannot in every case satisfy all sexual desires. On the other hand, it is difficult to see how any other form of marriage could, in the long run, meet the modern demands for personal **love** and trust, emotional security, and sexual equality. Nevertheless, under the circumstances, a certain degree of tolerance towards the so-called "illegitimate" forms of sexual activity seems both humane and practical.

morning-after pill   See **birth control.**

mother   A **woman** who has given **birth.**

The words "mother," "motherly," and "motherhood" usually have connotations of loving, caring, nurturing, and protecting children. However, the biological fact of a woman's motherhood does not guarantee that she will also develop motherly feelings. Sometimes, particularly in the case of an **unwanted pregnancy,** a mother may be unable to establish the necessary affectionate relationship with her baby. Fortunately, such cases are rare, and most mothers give their children all the love and attention they need for a healthy **sexual development.** However, it is also possible that, in time, such motherly love can become over-protective and possessive, eventually doing more harm than good.

Modern medicine and child psychology can now provide a mother with an adequate understanding of her child's needs, and thus enable her to strike a reasonable balance in her protective and educational efforts. These efforts can also be greatly helped if the child's **father** shares the mother's responsibilities.

In a **patriarchy,** men usually do not participate in the education of small children, considering it an exclusively female occupation and duty. In fact, male-dominated societies tend to restrict women to the tasks of childcare and housekeeping. In compensation for such social discrimination, there is often a glorification of motherhood.

The complete **equality of the sexes** is likely to end this over-emphasis on a female biological function and to lead to the full social recognition of all women, whether they are mothers or not.

narcissism

An unconscious fixation on oneself and a sexual desire for one's own body.

According to Greek legend, Narcissus was a beautiful youth in love with himself who drowned admiring the reflection of his face in the water.

Every small child is narcissistic as long as he does not understand that his satisfaction (of being fed, for example) depends on another person. In some cases this attitude is carried over into adulthood. A truly narcissistic adult is emotionally immature and unable to establish deep personal relationships with others. However, a modest amount of narcissism, as expressed in personal cleanliness and in care for one's well-being and appearance, is necessary and healthy.

natural childbirth

A term sometimes used for a physical and psychological technique which greatly reduces the pain of giving **birth** by an adequate preparation and active participation of the expectant mother.

The method of "natural childbirth" was first advanced by Dr. G. D. Read, a British obstetrician, who also developed a program of exercises designed to train the expectant mother in controlling her muscles. The final objective of these exercises is to make childbirth a process in which the mother, instead of playing an unpleasant passive role, can actively participate.

It seems that, in many cases, the major cause of pain during childbirth is a kind of spontaneous resistance to the process of birth. This resistance manifests itself in fear and muscular tension. It is also possible that certain other psychological factors, such as feelings of guilt or resentment, are involved in this kind of resistance. The end of a **pregnancy** is sometimes felt to be the unpleasant consequence of the pleasant experience called sexual intercourse. Some women may feel that a pregnancy puts a burden on them, while men can enjoy sexual pleasure without responsibility. Very often, of course, simple ignorance about the process of birth can cause apprehension at its arrival.

These and similar difficulties can be overcome by proper instruction, **family planning,** the use of **birth control,** and, generally, by understanding and cooperation between the sexes. Thus, the birth of a child can become a welcome opportunity for both parents to share a unique experience. Many modern obstetricians today train expectant mothers in the method of natural childbirth, and many hospitals allow, and indeed encourage, husbands to remain with their wives throughout the process of birth.

necking

Colloquial term used to describe kisses and caresses without complete bodily contact, and avoiding strong sexual excitement.

new morality

The new morality has one highest value: human understanding. It therefore attempts to meet every individual on his own terms, helping him to make the best of his particular situation.

The old morality has another highest value: divine law. It regulates all human behavior according to the same unalterable divine commands. The new morality differentiates between two attitudes: the first is the attitude of insensitive people who use and abuse each other as mere objects. The second is the attitude of truly human beings, who live together as brothers, and who need freedom and love. In short, the moral opposites are: blind rigidity versus understanding tolerance.

The old morality also differentiates between two attitudes: the first is the attitude of disobedient people who refuse to submit to the divine norm. The second is the attitude of truly obedient children of God who follow his eternal commandments. Thus the moral opposites are: rebellion versus obedience.

The old morality must be tested in the light of the new morality. Without this control it can easily become inhuman and cruel. Obedience to rigid norms and disregard for human beings have all too often gone hand in hand. (See also **sexual ethics, sin.**)

nocturnal emission
(See **sexual dream.**)

Ejaculation of **semen** during sleep. Also known in popular language as "wet dream."

nuclear family

Family consisting of only two successive generations: parents and children.

The smallest nuclear family consists of only two persons: mother and child. But even parents with many children form nothing more than a nuclear family as long as no further relatives (grandparents, aunts, uncles, cousins) are part of their household. (See **extended family.**)

The nuclear family is the result of social developments which have their roots in general technological changes as well as in the demands for greater individual freedom, independence, and privacy. However, the nuclear family has several disadvantages:

■ Since few persons share expensive appliances (kitchen, washer, dryer, refrigerator, tv, car, lawnmower), there is a certain amount of waste that increases the cost of living.

- The functions of father and mother tend to become totally separated. The father works outside of the house and is unavailable to his children most of the time. The mother, on the other hand, is tied to her household and the children, and has to give up most of her cultural, intellectual, and professional ambitions. This further enhances her husband's privileged position. (See **patriarchy.**)

All of this can result in serious problems, including sexual problems.

nudism A world-wide movement which advocates a "natural" way of life with much physical exercise in the open air, and without the restrictions of clothing. For this reason, nudists usually form private clubs and build their own camps, where they spend much of their free time in complete nudity without interference from others.

The nudist philosophy rejects many of our laws and social **conventions** concerning dress. For a nudist, they are expressions of an unhealthy, exaggerated sense of **modesty** and **fear** of the body. In contrast, nudists maintain that, in the natural state of nudity, people become more beautiful, more relaxed, and, ultimately, more humane. This philosophy is expounded in nudist magazines, which usually carry pictures of nude men, women, and children whose appearance is supposed to suggest the nudist ideal.

It is a moot question whether the nudist philosophy is hypocritical or sincere, sophisticated or simple-minded, reasonable or foolish. Basically, it is a matter of taste rather than rational argument.

Some people join a nudist group temporarily, or spend only their vacations at a nudist camp.

nudity Nudity reveals the human body as being sexually attractive as well as vulnerable and in need of protection.

The impression of nudity on the observer depends very much on his cultural background and on his education. Recent years have seen an increase of nudity in advertising, fashions, and entertainment. However, this does not necessarily mean that there has been an equal increase of sexual excitement in the viewer. In fact, some people complain that certain formerly hidden charms now no longer provide the expected stimulation.

Generally, the more open display of the nude body today can be considered a symptom of growing emotional maturity and of a more relaxed attitude towards human **sexuality.**

nymphomaniac A woman who feels a constant, extreme, and irrepressible desire for sexual satisfaction.

Very often women are falsely considered nymphomaniacs because they show a strong need for affection. Occasionally, sexually licentious behavior can occur within the context or as a symptom of certain psychological disorders. However, there is some doubt whether nymphomania as such really exists. It may very well be nothing but a male fantasy. (See also **double standard.**)

121

obscene Anything that is believed to violate the prevailing standards of sexual propriety. (See **sex legislation.**)

Apart from considerable theoretical difficulties, the problem of obscenity raises a number of practical questions. To begin with, there is no general agreement as to what the standards of sexual propriety actually are. Different people hold widely divergent views on the subject. But even where there is no doubt about the standards, there is usually a great deal of discussion as to whether they have, in fact, been violated. For instance, it is claimed that a work of art or scholarship can, by definition, never be obscene, no matter how shocking it may appear to some people. This argument often shifts the debate to the question of whether a certain book of film is art or not. However, art is, if anything, even more difficult to define than obscenity. These frustrating disputations are then often settled in court by means of some judicial decision that leaves at least one, and often all the contestants unconvinced. (See **pornography.**)

Under the circumstances, it would appear sensible to leave such questions to the individual, as long as he does not actually force his personal taste on others who do not care for it. The demand to be left alone in such cases seems reasonable enough. However, it is questionable whether people who themselves can easily avoid exposure to what they might consider obscene really need the protection of the police.

Oedipus complex A psychoanalytic term used in the interpretation of a certain unconscious crisis in a child's **sexual development.** The child's experiences and reactions during this so-called Oedipal phase largely determine his later ability to establish intimate contact with others.

The term "Oedipus complex" alludes to the legendary Greek king Oedipus who unknowingly killed his father and married his mother. This allusion seems justified by the following observation:

It is the rule for a young child to be actively interested in a person of the other sex. If we examine the behavior of a 4-year-old boy, for example, we discover that he is in love with a woman—his mother. She is, for him, the only woman he knows and cares to know. However, this woman already has a husband—the father. The boy is jealous of him and would like to push him aside in order to assume his position. This desire is usually expressed openly and spontaneously, as for instance when the boy climbs into his mother's bed announcing: "When I grow up, I'll marry you."

Obviously, this situation can be compared to that of King Oedipus, although there is one important difference: Oedipus actually did remove his father forever from his mother's side, and he did marry her. The normal development of a child takes another course:

The boy replaces his desire to marry his mother with the wish to marry a woman like his mother, and his urge to take the place of his father turns into the determination to become a man like his father. The boy can make this transition easily, if the father provides an attractive model to follow, and if he actively encourages his son to become a man. At the same time, it is the mother's task to help her son realize that she has already chosen and is no longer available as a sexual object. These parental attitudes will lead the boy to seek his sexual gratification elsewhere.

(In the case of a girl, the development takes the opposite course: she loves her father and is jealous of her mother. The respective psychoanalytic term is "Electra complex," after Electra, a legendary Greek princess who, after the death of her beloved father, helped kill her mother, who had murdered him.)

These unconscious experiences are very important for the developing child, who thus learns to find the proper attitude towards his parents. In doing so, he also develops his own sexual identity.

It follows from these observations that the way in which the parents treat each other as sexual partners, and how they talk about sexual matters, deeply influence the child's sexual development. It is therefore quite appropriate that young boys and young girls should become aware of their parents' relationship.

In overcoming the Oedipal crisis, a child will eventually look for a comparable relationship with a playmate. This is the time when parents may discover their children "playing doctor," exploring each other's bodies, or even masturbating each other. Parents who find themselves confronted with these situations should provide their children with an adequate explanation which puts such behavior in its proper perspective. After all, in their childlike way, the children do nothing else than what the adults do in an adult way.

oldest profession in the world

Euphemism for **prostitution.**

onanism

(After Onan, a biblical character who "spilled his seed on the ground.") An old-fashioned term for **coitus interruptus.** Occasionally, the term is also used in reference to **masturbation.**

125

oral intercourse

Sexual intercourse involving the mouth of one sexual partner and the **genitals** of the other. (See **cunnilingus, fellatio.**)

orgasm

Term normally used to describe the climax of **sexual pleasure. Satisfaction** of sexual **excitement,** followed by general physical relaxation.

Orgasm is a highly complicated physical process, usually accompanied by involuntary movements, sounds, and gestures, such as convulsions of the body, groans, and sighs. Orgasm can make the sexual partners oblivious to their surroundings and even to each other. In fact, it could be said that during orgasm they deeply feel and forget each other at the same time. In the male, orgasm is connected with his **ejaculation** of **semen.** There are also certain decisive physical movements in the female (particularly vaginal and other muscular contractions).

In order to reach orgasm, most women depend on uninterrupted coital movements after a certain degree of excitement has been reached. A man, on the other hand, might need to interrupt his movements in order to synchronize his own reactions with those of his partner. It is therefore important that both partners be sensitive to each other's needs. Some couples understand each other silently; others freely express their feelings in words in order to achieve greater physical harmony. It is this total communication, not **coitus** alone, that gives **sexual intercourse** its truly intimate character.

There is a belief that the most perfect coitus is one that results in simultaneous orgasm of both partners. However, this should not be considered the decisive criterion for satisfactory intercourse or a happy sexual relationship.

orgy

A gathering at which people have sexual intercourse with each other.

Originally, orgies had a religious function. On certain occasions (fertility rites), general public sexual intercourse was considered an appropriate offering to the gods.

Today the word "orgy" has mostly negative connotations. This is an indication of how much our attitude towards sex has been changed in the process of civilization. At one time in the past, sexual intercourse was something good that could be practiced openly. Today it is generally associated with feelings of guilt, shame, exclusiveness, and secrecy. Consequently, those engaging in it have to retreat from public view, and the discovery of their activities can easily create a scandal. Since the reasons for this negative attitude cannot be found in sexuality itself, they must be attributed to social and cultural factors. (See also **group sex, prudery.**)

ovaries

Two almond-sized glandular organs, one on each side of the **uterus**, which produce the ova. (See **ovum.**) They also produce **hormones** which influence the development of a woman's secondary **sexual characteristics**. In their function, the ovaries correspond to a man's **testicles**. The removal or loss of both ovaries results in **infertility**.

ovulation

The process by which the ripe egg (see **ovum**) is released from the **ovaries,** after which it travels through one of the **Fallopian tubes** into the uterus.

In a sexually mature woman, ovulation occurs fairly regularly about every 28 days, except during **pregnancy** and shortly after she has given **birth**. At the time of ovulation there is a slight rise in body temperature. (See **basal temperature.**)

ovum

(plural: ova) Egg. The female reproductive cell produced in the **ovaries**. An ovum is about 1/200 of an inch in diameter.

A woman's ovaries contain several hundred thousand potential ova, although only a few hundred are actually involved in the reproductive phase of her life. During the period between **puberty** and **menopause,** one egg ripens approximately every 28 days. (See **ovulation.**) The fertilization of an egg by a sperm cell (see **spermatozoa**) marks the beginning of a **pregnancy**.

The human ovum was not discovered until the 19th century.

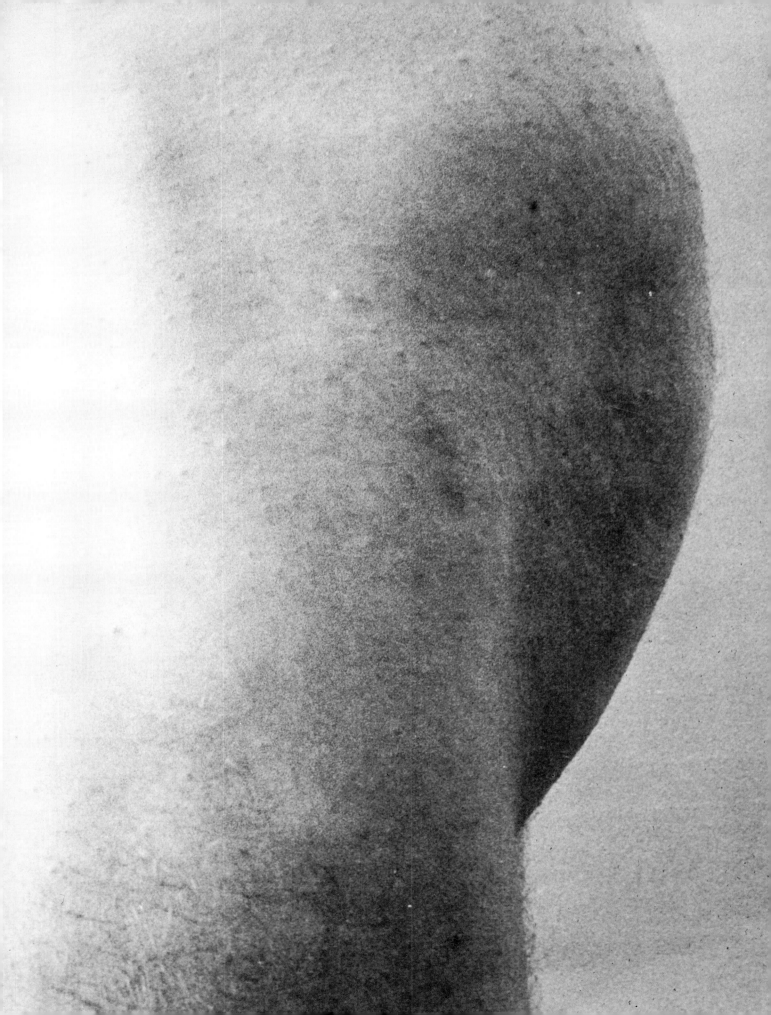

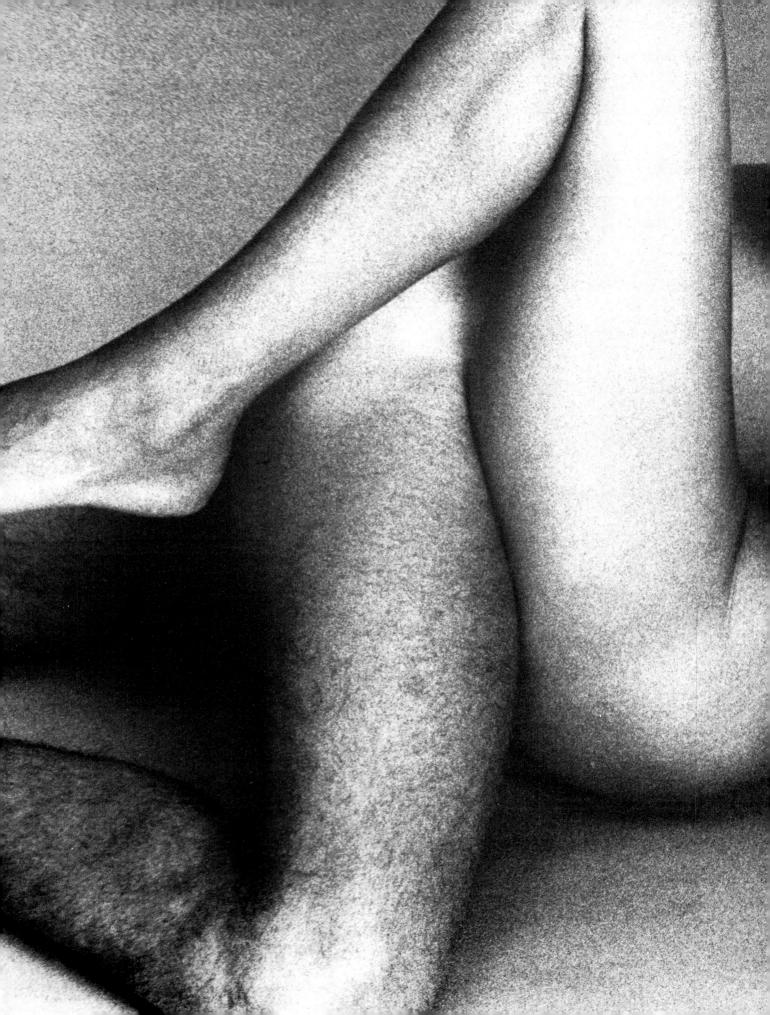

pansexualism (sometimes also "pansexuality") All-embracing sexual **love**. An attitude or a philosophy which is based on the belief that the human **sex drive** can and should be directed towards everybody and everything.

At one time, the term "pansexualism" was also used for the theory that all human behavior is somehow sexually motivated. This theory is no longer considered valid.

Today the terms "pansexualism" and "pansexuality" are often employed by certain advocates of sexual liberation who want to convey the idea that the **sexual roles** of men and women are too confining and that, therefore, labels such as "heterosexuality" and "homosexuality" should be abolished. It is doubtful, however, whether this usage will in the long run prove meaningful and practical.

passion A feeling, an urge, or a desire which sweeps away normal restraints and inhibitions in search of new experiences. More specifically, the expectation that, during sexual intercourse, the partner should be carried away to the point of **ecstasy**.

There are people who always expect instant and never-ending passion from their sexual partners. Such exaggerated expectations can usually be traced back to super-human models in books and movies. In real life, passionate feelings most often arise unexpectedly, and under unusual circumstances. No man and no woman can be passionate all the time.

Occasionally sexual partners can impair their relationship by an attempt to recreate former moments of passion, instead of trying to explore new possibilities. (See also **variety.**)

paternity Fatherhood. The state or condition of being a **father.**

132

paternity suit A legal suit aimed at determining the father of an **illegitimate child**. Such a suit is usually filed in order to secure financial support for the child.

patriarchy A form of society in which all important decisions are made by men.

In a patriarchal society men dominate most spheres of life, such as politics, administration, economy, science, art, and religion. They also enjoy a privileged position sexually. (See **masculinity, femininity, man, woman, double standard, emancipation, equality of the sexes.**)
There have been attempts to compensate for the discrimination against women by showing special respect for their roles as young, "innocent" girls, virgins, wives, and mothers (Mother's Day). Today such attempts are no longer convincing. In fact, many women regard them as insincere and even offensive, while many men have begun to realize that there is no substitute for true sexual equality. Most Western countries today are still more or less patriarchal. There is usually only one main area where male influence is weak or even absent: the education of small children, which has become the almost exclusive right and obligation of women. However, this social arrangement is hardly ideal. (See **father.**)
In the course of history, there were also cultures dominated by women. (See **matriarchy.**)
In the modern world, the effective use and control of technology depends less and less on typically "masculine" or "feminine" attitudes and approaches. Thus for the first time in history there is now a need and an opportunity to develop new forms of partnership between men and women.

pederasty Sexual relationship between an adult man and a male adolescent.

In our culture, all sexual relationships between adults and **minors** are considered socially harmful. Pederasty, being a **homosexual** relationship, meets with particularly strong disapproval. It is illegal in the United States as well as in many other countries.

However, it is known that, occasionally, certain societies have taken a different view. In ancient Greece, for example, pederasty often had a general educational function, and was socially approved for this reason.

Occasionally, the term "pederasty" is also falsely used as a synonym for **anal intercourse.**
Pederasty should not be confounded with pedophilia, a sexual **perversion.**

peeping Tom Colloquial term for **voyeur.** (See **perversion.**)

penilingus Fellatio.

penis The male sex organ. Part of the male external **genitals**, consisting of some sponge-like erectile tissue and a bulb-like extremity called **glans.**

The glans, which is very sensitive to the touch, is covered by the **foreskin** and contains an opening which marks the end of the **urethra** (the tract through which the urine is released). During **ejaculation**, the **semen** also passes through the same opening.

The penis, which usually remains in a soft and flaccid condition, stiffens and increases in size as its hollow erectile tissue is filled with blood during sexual **excitement**. In this state of **erection**, the penis can be introduced into the **vagina** for the purpose of **coitus.**

The erect penis has long been considered a symbol of strength and fertility. (See **phallus.**) Some people also believe the size of the penis to be an indication of sexual **potency**. However, this belief is erroneous. Neither is the size of the penis decisive for the satisfaction of sexual partners.

period A term sometimes used for **menstruation.**

perversion A psychological disorder impeding the capacity for full sexual contact and response, and resulting in some sort of compulsive and frustrating behavior.

The term "perversion" (just as "aberration," "deviation," or "abnormality") implies the transgression of a certain norm for sexual behavior. The concrete definition of this norm is usually left to the religious, legal, and medical authorities. As seen from their particular points of view, a violation of the norm is either a sin, a crime, or a disease, and the word "perversion" has been used to mean any of these things. However, the various religious, legal, and medical definitions are subject to change and do not necessarily agree with each other. (See **aberration, unnatural sex.**)

As far as the general public is concerned, there is a tendency to call every sexual act perverse that is unfamiliar. People who engage in such acts are just as readily called perverts. In everyday language, therefore, the word "perverse" often means nothing more than "strange and disgusting."

From a clinical point of view, it seems sensible to restrict the use of the term "perversion" to sexual behavior that is compulsive, exclusive, destructive, or accompanied by feelings of guilt and anxiety. In other words, a patient suffers from a perversion when his sexual desire is tied to a certain kind of compulsive behavior, which, nevertheless, fails to give him the full amount of physical and emotional satisfaction of which he would be capable otherwise. He is unable to relate to his sexual partners as persons, meet them on their own terms, respond to their individual sexual needs, or to adapt his own sexual behavior to different circumstances and situations. He cannot love. Instead, in his search for sexual gratification, he is condemned to an almost ritualistic repetition of the same frustrating acts. In this sense, a perversion is like an addiction. Men and women who suffer from a perversion are sick and should seek professional help.

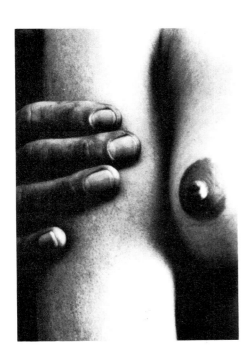

Examples of sexual perversions are:

SADISM (named after the Marquis de Sade, an 18th-century French writer). A sadist, in order to be sexually aroused and satisfied, needs to inflict physical or mental pain on his sexual partner. In extreme cases, this kind of compulsive cruelty can lead to murder.

MASOCHISM (named after Sacher-Masoch, a 19th-century Austrian writer). A masochist, in order to be sexually aroused and satisfied, needs a partner who inflicts pain on him. Masochists will ask to be humiliated, abused, beaten, and even tortured by their partners.

VOYEURISM A voyeur, in order to be sexually aroused and satisfied, needs to watch other people taking their clothes off, masturbating, or having sexual intercourse.

EXHIBITIONISM An exhibitionist, in order to be sexually aroused and satisfied, needs other people to look at his genitals, or watch him masturbate.

PEDOPHILIA A pedophile is unable to enjoy the responses of a sexually mature person. Instead, he is sexually aroused only by children.

TRANSVESTISM A transvestite, in order to be sexually aroused and satisfied, needs to disguise himself. He does not want to be loved the way he is. Instead, he enacts the role of a member of the opposite sex, or pretends to be a baby, or an animal, or some other creature or object.

FETISHISM A fetishist, in order to be sexually aroused and satisfied, does not desire another person, but rather a part of him, or an object which belongs to him, such as a shoe, or a dress, or some hair. Such an object (the fetish) can even be totally unrelated to a particular person.

COPROPHILIA A coprophile, in order to be sexually aroused and satisfied, needs to play with excrement.

ZOOPHILIA or BESTIALITY A zoophile is unable to respond to human sexual partners. Instead, he prefers animals, such as sheep, dogs, horses, and cows.

NECROPHILIA A necrophile cannot respond to any living sexual partners. Instead, he is sexually aroused by dead bodies.

Most perversions never become manifest in public, since they occur between married couples. After all, the majority of people today are married, and in the long run it is impossible to hide one's true sexual tendencies from a marriage partner. If the partner refuses to cooperate, the one who suffers from a perversion is likely to seek relief elsewhere, often from **prostitutes.** Sometimes the lack of willing partners can lead him to acts of public indecency, and make him a **sex offender.** On the other hand, some perversions (such as fetishism) can be satisfied without partners.

The problem of perversion is a complex one. In many respects, it is a matter of degree rather than substance.
The human sexual drive consists of a number of partial drives whose eventual proper balance is the basis for any responsible sexual behavior. This balance is the result of the process of sexual maturation. A newborn child is totally dominated by its physical and emotional needs.

135

His sexuality is still unfocused. In the course of his **sexual development**, the partial drives become manifest in several phases. The sequence of these phases provides us with hints of almost all perversions. These hints are indications of sexual growth. The child's sexual growth continues through various more or less active stages until, finally, the partial drives achieve their balance during puberty.

This observation leads to the conclusion that so-called perversions in adults are the result of an imbalance due to arrested sexual development. The causes for this imbalance are adverse influences during infancy and childhood. In other words, some psychological obstacle has prevented the growing personality from developing its full capacity for love.

There are, of course, many shades and degrees of arrested sexual development. The resulting imbalance can therefore manifest itself in many different ways. The term "perversion" is appropriate only where this imbalance has led to some sort of compulsive behavior and emotional self-isolation.

Insight into the origin of perversions is indispensable for an understanding of human sexuality. Everything we know about this subject today compels us to consider perverse sexual behavior as a symptom of sickness rather than a crime. People who commit perverse acts do not belong in prison, but should receive professional medical treatment.

Our understanding of human sexual development also implies the knowledge that, to a certain extent, we all share the basic tendencies which the so-called perversions present in their extreme form.

Some sadistic impulses, for instance, are part of almost everybody's sexual behavior. They can express themselves in particularly passionate and inconsiderate embraces, by biting and scratching during intercourse, and generally by all forms of brutality, and by the will to dominate. Masochistic tendencies become apparent in the form of passivity and submission. Most people are also familiar with the basic impulse of voyeurism, as they enjoy looking at the body of a potential sexual partner, or like to watch nude men and women in movies or in magazines. Certain fashions, on the other hand, respond to our exhibitionistic tendencies. The limits of the permissible usually vary considerably from one time and place to another. In the United States today it ranges from the mini-skirt and the bikini for the average girl and woman to "topless" and "bottomless" waitresses in bars. A vestige of fetishism can be detected in the collection of autographs, love letters, or other personal memorabilia, such as a lock of hair, or a handkerchief. The same tendency appears in an obsession with some parts of the female or male anatomy, such as the breasts or the buttocks. Most people also unconsciously express tendencies of zoophilia by giving their partners the names of animals such as tiger, pussycat, chick, and so on. Inclinations towards transvestism become manifest at such occasions as costume balls, parades, or in dramatic art (the ever popular play "Charley's Aunt" is a typical example).

The individual combination of all these various partial drives gives everybody his own unique sexual identity and appeal. It also determines his preference for certain sexual partners. As long as these drives retain their proper balance, they provide for a wide range of rewarding responses and contribute to a fuller enjoyment of our sexuality.

pessary A term sometimes used for the **cervical cap** or, less frequently, for the **diaphragm.**

petting Intimate caresses and close physical contact between sexual partners including the touching of the genitals, but avoiding **copulation.**

Petting is a special form of **sexual intercourse** common among young people who try to find a compromise between their private desire for sexual gratification and the public demand for their sexual **abstinence.** (See **premarital intercourse.**)

Traditionally, it was the woman who had to prove her premarital abstinence by preserving her **virginity.** The **wedding night** was the time of her **defloration**, and the husband expected to find his wife's **hymen** intact when he "took possession" of her. This so-called "technical virginity" was considered sufficient evidence of her sexual "innocence."

This line of reasoning finally led to the belief that some sort of premarital intercourse was permissible even for women, as long as the actual insertion of the **penis** into the **vagina** was avoided. Consequently, there are many adults today who are willing to tolerate petting between young people even to the point of mutual **masturbation.** However, there are also others who object to the practice on the ground that it will invariably lead to **coitus**, which should be reserved for marriage. Still others point out that petting is, at best, a frustrating exercise and, at worst, a hypocritical tribute to the sexual **double standard.**

Nevertheless, all things considered, it seems that petting can be defended as an intermediate phase in a growing sexual relationship. At the same time, it has to be admitted that, in the long run, this kind of restricted intercourse is unsatisfactory as the only form of sexual expression.

phallus (Greek: phallos) **Penis.** Today the term "phallus" is most often used for the artistic representation of a penis in the state of **erection.**

In ancient Greece and Rome, the erect phallus was a symbol of life and fertility. Its image was openly displayed in public. There were, for instance, statues of phallic deities, such as Hermes and Priapus, which were believed to protect the lives of travellers or to insure a good harvest. The phallus symbol was also worn in the form of jewellery, as a good-luck charm.

It was not until after the rise of Christianity that people began to take offense at the artistic representation of genitals. This new **prudery** resulted in the curious practice of covering the genitals of classical Greek and Roman statues with biblical fig leaves.

phimosis Tightness of the **foreskin**, requiring its surgical removal. (See **circumcision.**)

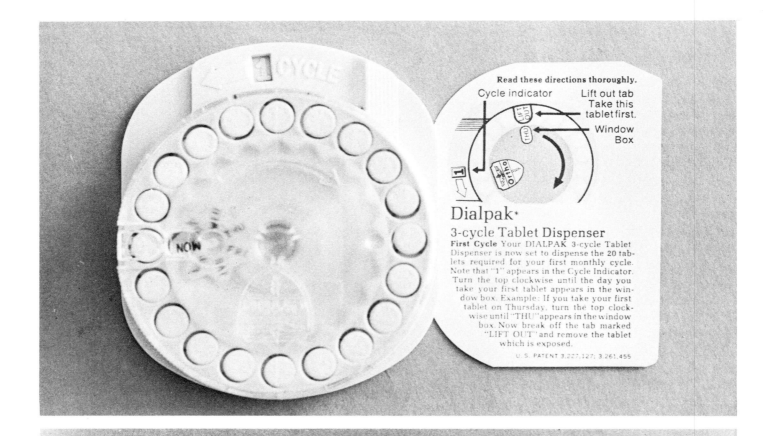

Read these directions thoroughly.

Cycle indicator — Lift out tab Take this tablet first.

Window Box

Dialpak*
3-cycle Tablet Dispenser

First Cycle Your DIALPAK 3-cycle Tablet Dispenser is now set to dispense the 20 tablets required for your first monthly cycle. Note that "1" appears in the Cycle Indicator. Turn the top clockwise until the day you take your first tablet appears in the window box. Example: If you take your first tablet on Thursday, turn the top clockwise until "THU" appears in the window box. Now break off the tab marked "LIFT OUT" and remove the tablet which is exposed.

U.S. PATENT 3,227,127; 3,261,455

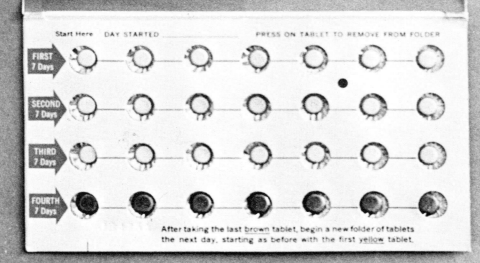

NORLESTRIN® Fe 1 mg.

Each yellow tablet contains:
norethindrone acetate 1 mg.
ethinyl estradiol 0.05 mg.

Each brown tablet contains:
ferrous fumarate, U.S.P., 75 mg.

(Place prescription label here.)

DIRECTIONS:

1. The first day of your period is Day 1. On the fifth day (Day 5), start taking one yellow tablet daily, beginning with the tablet marked "Start Here." In the space provided, write the day you start.

2. On the day after taking the last yellow tablet, begin taking one brown tablet daily until they are gone.

Without interruption, begin each new folder by taking the yellow tablets first, followed by the brown tablets. There should never be a day when you are not taking a tablet. Always have another folder ready to begin when one is finished.

Your period should begin while you are taking the brown tablets. Even if your period does not occur, CONTINUE TAKING YOUR TABLETS AS DIRECTED.

Start Here   DAY STARTED _____   PRESS ON TABLET TO REMOVE FROM FOLDER

FIRST 7 Days

SECOND 7 Days

THIRD 7 Days

FOURTH 7 Days

After taking the last brown tablet, begin a new folder of tablets the next day, starting as before with the first yellow tablet.

pill More specifically: birth-control pill. The safest and most reliable means of **birth control**.

Birth-control pills contain certain synthetic hormones which resemble those produced by the female body during **pregnancy** and which suppress **ovulation**. In other words, the pills cause a kind of false pregnancy, thus preventing the occurrence of a real one. However, the amount of hormones contained in the pills is less than 1% of that released during an actual pregnancy.

The pills are taken regularly each day for 20 or 21 days, starting on the 5th day after the first day of **menstruation**. Within 3–5 days after the last pill has been taken, menstrual bleeding occurs again, thus resulting in a menstrual cycle of about 28 days. However, a one-time absence of such bleeding is not necessarily a symptom of pregnancy, and the use of pills can be continued according to the usual schedule. Should a woman forget to take the pill, she can catch up within 36 hours by taking an additional pill. After a lapse of more than 36 hours, the contraceptive effect of the pills becomes doubtful, and the woman should, after an interim of 6 or 7 days, start all over again, or follow the advice of her doctor.

Since the effect of the pills depends on their regular use, they should be taken each day at the same time as part of the daily routine. This will also keep a stable hormonal level within the body.

The pills may produce some minor side effects similar to those of a pregnancy, such as nausea, dizziness, backache, or an enlargement of the breasts. These side effects usually disappear after some time. In some cases it may also be necessary to switch to another brand of pills with a slightly different chemical composition.

Before using the pill, every woman should ask for and follow the advice of her doctor. Occasionally, medical reasons may compel a doctor to advise against the use of the pill and to prescribe a different method of birth control.

pimp A man who forces a woman to become a **prostitute**, or who helps her to procure business and who profits from her prostitution.

Very often a pimp takes advantage of girls who find themselves in desperate circumstances. In other cases, prostitutes welcome the protection and experience of a pimp, and do not object to sharing their income with him.

Planned Parenthood

The International Planned Parenthood Federation is a worldwide organization composed of **family planning** organizations from 64 nations which helps provide voluntary **birth control** services in more than 100 countries.

The Planned Parenthood Federation of America, Inc., which offers the the same services to Americans, has its headquarters in New York and several regional offices around the country. There are also affiliated committees and councils in every state of the union. The respective offices are listed in the telephone book of almost every large city.

Platonic love

A love of the soul, not of the body, a deep affection for somebody's personality, without sexual desire.

The term was originally used for a certain kind of **homosexual** love. The ancient Greek philosopher Plato, in his "Symposium," has Socrates describe his feelings for Alcibiades, a beautiful young man, whose sexual advances he had rejected. Socrates proposes a "higher," non-physical form of love that aspires, above everything else, to a union of souls.

polygamy

Marriage between more than two partners.

Usually, polygamy means that a man has several wives. (In some Islamic countries a man has as many as four wives, in some African and East Asian countries an unlimited number.) In some cultures of the past polygamy meant one woman having several husbands.

Since, in our culture, **monogamy** is the only legal form of marriage, many people feel that it should become universal. However, in societies where polygamy has been a way of life for many centuries, monogamy cannot be legally or morally imposed upon the population from one day to the other. Obviously, the entire social structure has to be changed. Even where this should appear desirable, it will take considerable time and patience. A non-Christian husband, for instance, who lives in polygamy, can encounter severe moral problems by converting to Christianity. He then has to choose one of his wives to remain as his spouse and dismiss the others. These rejected women find themselves suddenly without the protection of a home, without family, and without any means of support. There is also the problem of custody of the children.

However, monogamy is not merely a Christian dogma and a Western custom. It has also often been demanded by non-Westerners and non-Christians in the interest of sexual equality. Still, wherever it replaces polygamy, the period of transition is bound to be difficult. Its problems can be solved only with a great deal of tact, tolerance, and circumspection.

Occasionally, one enounters the argument that man is naturally polygamous. In other words, it is said that man is not made to restrict his sexual interest to one sexual partner all his life. Certainly, the mere fact that someone is engaged or married does not make him lose sexual interest in other people. It takes a personal decision to renounce all sexual relationships but one. However, this decision can and will be made when the love for one's partner requires it.

pornography

(From Greek "porne": whore, and "graphein": to write) A term used by certain people for pictures, statues, books, or films that depict nudity or sexual activity in a fashion of which they disapprove.

This formal definition implies a lack of objective criteria for pornography, and indeed no consensus has ever been reached on the matter. No policeman, lawyer, or judge has ever been able to come up with a generally accepted definition. Neither have artists and critics ever agreed on this

point. Nevertheless, there seems to be some sort of understanding among all experts that it is somehow typical for pornography to stimulate sexual **excitement** in the viewer or reader. However, the same experts totally disagree about the effects of this excitement. Some take it for granted that the effects are harmful; others believe them to be beneficial. It is not surprising, therefore, that definitions of what is pornographic and the restrictions placed upon pornography differ considerably from one time and culture to another. At present, some countries (such as the Soviet Union) have very harsh and extensive restrictions, while others have very little (Sweden, Germany). One country (Denmark) has no restrictions at all. So far, there have not been any extensive and conclusive studies comparing the experiences of these various countries.

In the United States there is a variety of laws and regulations which, although constantly challenged in court, try to control pornography, even if they can do so only in a capricious and haphazard fashion.

For example, some states or cities allow certain sex-films to be shown, as long as no **erections** are visible. On the whole, it seems that many people consider male nudity to be more pornographic than female nudity. The reasons for this curious attitude are not entirely clear. It could be an expression of **male supremacy** or fear of **homosexuality**. There is also a general uneasiness about showing nude people touching each other. Furthermore, there are usually strong objections to the depiction of sexual pleasure, excitement, or ecstasy. Such things can be printed or shown only if they are "redeemed" by some other "social value." In other words, it is believed that **sexual pleasure** itself does not represent such a value. This belief can only be attributed to private and public **prudery**.

Some people are particularly concerned about possible negative effects of pornography on children and teenagers. However, there is no scientific proof that sexually explicit material is in fact harmful to children. (There is also no proof that it is beneficial.) Understandably, the authorities are reluctant to conduct the necessary practical experiments. However, in view of the fact that the concept of what is pornographic varies from culture to culture, and even from group to group within the same culture, it is unlikely that any final truth is ever going to be discovered in this area. The problem of pornography is basically one of cultural attitudes towards sex. Historically and geographically, such attitudes range from total condemnation to total acceptance. There have been cultures to which the very concept of pornography was completely unknown, and where, without apparent negative consequences, children from their earliest ages were exposed to all manifestations of human sexuality.

On the other hand, it is obvious that, in our own culture, sexual as well as other matters can be presented in a gross, tactless, tasteless, and even revolting fashion. It is doubtful, however, whether legal restrictions against pornography are an appropriate way of dealing with this problem. In 1970 the Federal Commission on Obscenity and Pornography, after extensive study, recommended the repeal of all laws that prohibit the sale, exhibition, or distribution of "pornography" to consenting adults. Indeed, it seems sensible to leave such matters to individual choice. If pornography has to be controlled at all, a proper and early **sex education** seems to be the most promising way to eliminate pornography or what are feared to be its evil effects. (See **obscene, sex legislation**.)

positions

During **coitus**, men and women can assume various coital positions, for example:

- The man lies on his back, facing the woman who straddles him, controlling the coital movements.

- The woman lies on her back, while the man, facing her, lies on top of her; his legs are placed between hers, and he controls the coital movements.

- Both partners lie on their side, the man behind the woman.

- Both partners lie on their side, facing each other.

The choice of any particular position depends on the preference and the mood of the sexual partners. Many couples choose different positions on different occasions in order to achieve **variety.** Certain positions allow for a deeper penetration of the penis into the vagina. This can increase the chance for a pregnancy. Some positions are also more convenient for women who are already pregnant. (See **sexual intercourse during pregnancy.)** Other positions may be chosen because the partners enjoy looking at each other, or because they want to caress certain parts of each other's bodies. In short, there are just as many different coital positions as reasons for choosing them.

There is no such thing as a "normal" position. Uninhibited and imaginative sexual partners who are sensitive enough to explore each other's **erogenous zones** discover new coital positions spontaneously without the help of **sex manuals.**

potency

Sexual ability of the male.

Actually, the term "potency" can refer to two different abilities:

- The ability to perform **coitus.** Potency in this sense is the ability to have and maintain an **erection** during sexual intercourse. The lack of this ability is called **impotence.**

- The ability to procreate. Potency in this sense is the man's ability to cause pregnancy in a woman. The lack of this ability is called **infertility** or **sterility.**

A man may lack the second of these abilities without lacking the first. In other words, it is possible for a man to be infertile without being impotent. (See also **sterilization.**)

It is also possible for a man to be impotent without being infertile. In such a case, he may still be able to father a child by means of **artificial insemination.**

pregnancy

The condition of a woman between the **conception** and **birth** of her baby.

The normal duration of a pregnancy is about 9 months or 280 days. During this period, the developing baby grows from an **embryo** to a viable **fetus.** At the same time, the future **mother** can prepare herself for her new role.

142

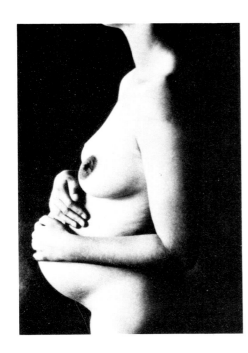

A woman who remembers the first day of her last menstruation before conception can estimate the date of delivery by means of a simple rule of thumb: "months minus 3; days plus 7." For example:

Last menstruation: December 10, or, in numerals, 12. 10.
Months minus 3:
12   −   3 = 9
Days plus   7:
10   +   7 = 17
Date of delivery: 9. 17. or September 17.

(See also **sexual intercourse during pregnancy, symptoms of pregnancy, unwanted pregnancy.**)

premarital intercourse

A term often used in reference to **sexual intercourse** between young people.

Since the term "premarital" refers to the period between **puberty** and **marriage,** it cannot be applied to the behavior of people who remain **single** throughout their lives. However, it is impossible to know beforehand who will eventually get married, and who will not. Strictly speaking, the term "premarital intercourse" is appropriate only in the case of a person who has definitely decided to marry. It also makes sense when used in retrospect by people who are married, and who look back on their sexual experiences before marriage. But even within these narrow logical limits, the term fails to make one important distinction: it applies indiscriminately not only to couples who are engaged, but also to couples who have no intention of marrying one another, yet who may, at some later date, get married to someone else.

It should be clear from these observations that the term "premarital intercourse," as commonly used, oversimplifies and prejudges the issue of sex between unmarried partners.

It seems that today most young people who engage in sexual intercourse do indeed seek a stable and affectionate relationship. However, such a relationship does not necessarily lead to marriage. In some cases, it may be no more than an expression of **friendship.** As personal and professional contacts between the sexes increase, so do the opportunities for more intimate relationships. Many young men and women welcome such opportunities for a deeper personal commitment.

Nevertheless, despite the new general climate of tolerance, sexual intercourse between unmarried partners can still create considerable problems:

■ Laws and statutes against fornication, seduction, statutory rape, crimes against nature, and so forth, although rarely enforced, technically still make criminals out of most unmarried people. (See **sex legislation.**)

■ Very often, the external circumstances are unfavorable. Young people who live with their parents, or in dormitories or rooming houses, usually do not have enough privacy for a sexual relationship.

■ Many young people are ignorant about the various methods of **birth control** and thus may risk an **unwanted pregnancy**.

- Because of a still prevailing **double standard**, the social consequences of sexual intercourse or the birth of an **illegitimate child** may be very different for men and women.

- Some young couples wrongly apply the standards of marriage to a relationship of **free love**. They expect too much, and are bound to be disappointed.

Sexual intercourse between unmarried partners usually meets with sharply divided opinions:

There are people who believe that all unmarried persons should lead a life of complete sexual **abstinence**. They feel that early sexual intercourse between young people cannot fail to corrupt their sense of responsibility, and will stunt their emotional growth. Indeed, many adults are convinced that sex without marriage will prevent a young person's emotional maturation and thus lead to moral decay.

A second opinion holds that such moral questions have to be decided according to the changing circumstances. The adherents of this view argue that every case has to be judged on its merits and that, in other words, sex between unmarried partners is sometimes right and sometimes wrong. Eventually, each individual has to make his own decision.

Finally, there are those who declare that sexual intercourse is good as such, and should not at all be restricted to marriage. In fact, they maintain that sexual intercourse is an excellent preparation for marriage, since it enables the partners to get to know each other better before they decide to stay together for life. It is further argued that single persons also have an unalienable right to sexual intercourse.

It seems that, today, it is the third of these opinions that is clearly gaining ground, although it stands in marked contrast to the teachings of most officially sanctioned **sex education**.

In view of these various contesting philosophies, it is impossible to provide generally binding recommendations. Most rules for sexual behavior are changeable and do change, because they do not depend on biological facts, but are rooted in cultural values. (See also **sexual ethics**.)

premature ejaculation

The term is used in cases where a man reaches **orgasm** sooner than desired.

Premature ejaculation can be a source of frustration. However, since its causes are mostly psychological, professional treatment can help. This treatment may consist of no more than a few technical instructions, since, in many cases, a simple manipulation known as "Seman's squeeze technique" can quickly improve the patient's condition.

prepuce

Medical term for **foreskin**.

promiscuity

Habitual sexual intercourse with more than one partner, either by frequently changing partners or by having relationships with several partners at the same time.

Promiscuity is often a symptom of emotional immaturity and the inability to establish deep and lasting personal contacts. The reason for such behavior is usually low self-esteem or some feeling of guilt.

Homosexuals are often promiscuous, because they have to hide their true sexual preference from their friends and therefore are forced to seek anonymous encounters, and because their families, employers, and landlords discourage them from openly and permanently living with one partner.

prophylactic   See **condom**.

prostitute
A person who engages in **sexual intercourse** in exchange for money. There are female and male prostitutes. (See **call girl, hooker, streetwalker,** and **hustler, stud.**)

For prostitutes sex is business. They normally do not get emotionally involved with their clients, but rather try to accommodate as many customers as possible, in order to increase their earnings. During intercourse they do not necessarily display any signs of affection or tenderness. Special requests, such as for longer company or for cooperation in **abnormal** sexual acts, are usually granted only in return for increased pay. Prostitutes generally use **contraceptives** or ask their customers to wear **condoms**. Some prostitutes suffer from infertility as a result of **venereal disease.**

Prostitution is often nothing more than an apparently easy way to make money. Occasionally, prostitutes are people with an underdeveloped capacity for personal contact and love. Some female postitutes, in fact, hate men. Others manage to give up prostitution and become responsible wives and mothers.

prostitution
Engaging in **sexual intercourse** in exchange for money.

Its most common form is female prostitution. Girls or women offer their sexual services in **brothels**, where they have to share their profits with the management, or they walk certain streets where they try to attract customers by appropriate modes of dress, make-up, or gestures. Even in these cases, prostitutes often share their income with **pimps.** These are male companions who give them advice, help them to procure business, and try to protect them from interference by the police. **Call girls** are prostitutes who take appointments by phone.

There are also male prostitutes. (See **hustler, stud.**) Some of them work as "private secretaries" or "travelling companions" for men or women, thus financing their travels or their education. Others work as "masseurs" or "models" for certain agencies, and can be called by phone for an appointment. Still others stand at street corners, at bus terminals, or in other public places in order to be picked up by strangers.

Prostitution has sometimes been called "the oldest profession in the world," meaning that it has always existed in the past, and among all nations. Occasionally, prostitution served a religious function, as in the case of so-called "temple prostitution." At other times, prostitution was a result of the sexual **double standard**. This standard, while allowing for some male sexual license, demanded total sexual abstinence of all women before and outside of marriage. It usually turned out that the virginity and chastity of "respectable" women could more easily be protected by providing the men with the opportunity to have sexual intercourse with prostitutes. In a way, then, prostitution was considered both evil and useful for society. It was the fight against this type of social hypocrisy (see   Shaw's play "Mrs. Warren's Profession") and the growing **emancipation** of women which helped to end the double standard in large parts of Europe and the United States.

Nevertheless, the social condemnation of prostitution has continued. It is illegal in the United States and in many other countries. (See **sex legislation**.) Certain countries, such as Germany, have legalized female heterosexual prostitution, but prohibit male heterosexual and homosexual prostitution. This legal inconsistency could be a relic of the double standard. Some countries, such as the Netherlands, have legalized both heterosexual and homosexual prostitution of adults.

Today, because of growing social honesty and tolerance in sexual matters, the extent of prostitution may have somewhat declined. On the other hand, no amount of legislation or public pressure has ever succeeded in eliminating it entirely. Apparently, few societies have yet been able to provide adequate sexual fulfillment for all of their citizens. As long as there is an otherwise unsatisfiable demand, prostitution is likely to continue providing the supply.

prudery Rejection of sexuality.

Prudery is a sign of a conscious or unconscious **fear** of sex. It can always be traced back to an inadequate **sex education**.

A prudish person has a low opinion of sex in general. He believes it to be over-emphasized by others, and feels threatened by its open discussion. If forced to talk about it, he will usually stress the procreational function of sex at the expense of its pleasurable aspects.

The fact that our language does not possess simple, commonly accepted terms for the various sexual activities is a result of general prudery. (See **Glossary of Sexual Slang** at end of present volume.)

The continued lack of early public sex education in large parts of the United States can also be ascribed to the prudery of some parents and educators.

Prudery and its opposite, sexual licentiousness, have the same cause: an inadequate understanding of sexuality, and of its potential for enriching our lives by providing positive and beneficial contacts between people.

puberty The period of life during which the **genitals** become capable of reproduction. (See **body.**)

Puberty normally arrives in the early teens (between the ages of 9–16 for girls and 11–18 for boys). On the average, girls reach puberty about two years earlier than boys. (See also **sexual development.**)

In our culture, boys and girls who reach puberty thereby enter a period of stress. (See **adolescence.**) One of the main sources of this stress is the fact that they are physically ready for **sexual intercourse,** but are denied it. (See also **abstinence, premarital intercourse.**) In some other cultures, where these restrictions do not exist, many of the emotional difficulties usually associated with puberty are also absent.

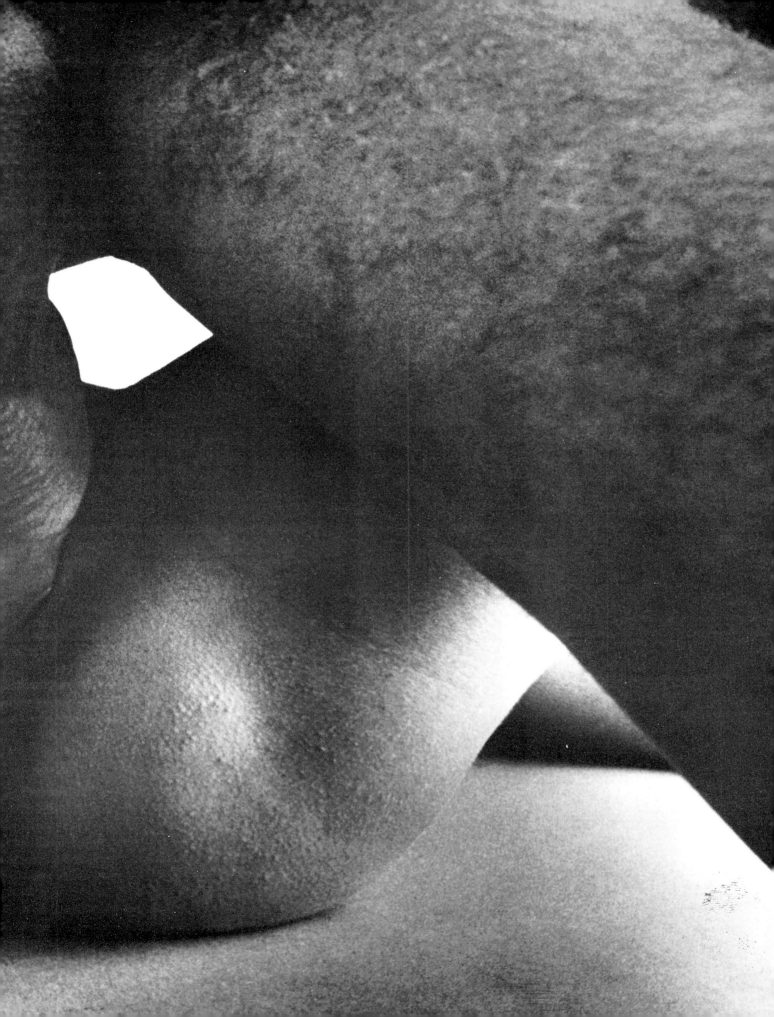

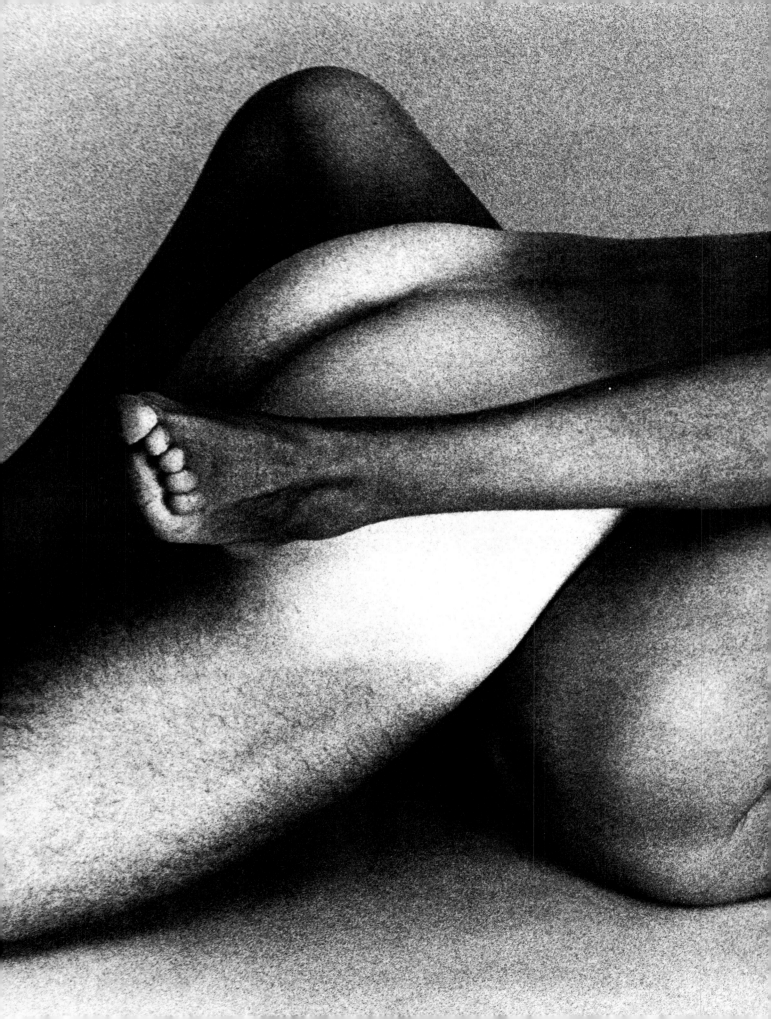

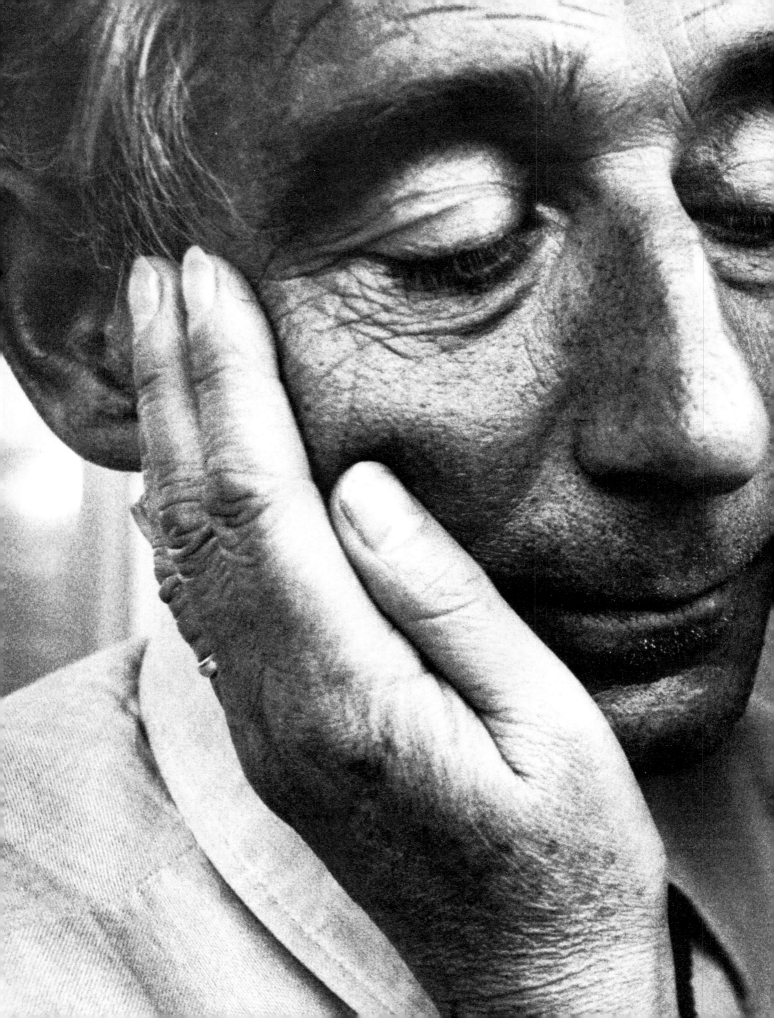

rape In everyday language, the word "rape" usually implies that a woman has been forced by a man (the rapist) to engage in sexual intercourse with him against her will. There are also cases (in prison, for example) where men rape other men.

As a legal term, "rape" has a broader meaning: sexual intercourse without the partner's lawful consent. (See **sex legislation.**)

reliability of birth control methods

In the course of one year, the following percentages of couples regularly engaging in sexual intercourse are likely to incur a pregnancy:

Method	Careful Use	Less Careful Use
none	60	
rhythm	15 —	40
spermicides	15 —	20
coitus interruptus	15 —	20
condom or **diaphragm**	12 —	14
condom or diaphragm plus spermicides	0 —	10
pill	0 —	3

These approximate figures have been compiled from various scientific sources. They can only show how much the different contraceptive methods vary in their effectiveness. (See **birth control.**)

Rh factor (Short for Rhesus factor) An antigen present in the blood of most people (about 85% of the white population in the United States). These people are therefore called Rh-positive. The remaining percentage of the population, who do not possess the Rh factor, are called Rh-negative.

156

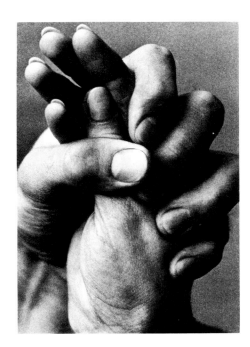

When an Rh-negative person receives a transfusion of Rh-positive blood, his blood plasma develops antibodies. These antibodies do not cause any harm unless a second transfusion of Rh-positive blood occurs, in which case the patient may experience severe reactions. A careful classification and separation of Rh-positive and Rh-negative blood types can help avoid such complications.

Problems can also arise when a woman with Rh-negative blood becomes pregnant by an Rh-positive man. In such a case, her developing baby is likely to be Rh-positive as well. However, when the Rh-positive blood of the **fetus** passes into the mother's circulation, her own Rh-negative blood forms antibodies which, in turn, enter the fetal bloodstream. In the case of a first pregnancy, this usually does not cause any harm, but later pregnancies may be adversely affected.

Today such conditions can usually be controlled by appropriate medical measures. It is therefore no longer inadvisable for an Rh-negative woman to marry an Rh-positive man.

rhythm method

The so-called rhythm method of **birth control** consists of temporary sexual **abstinence** during a woman's fertile period.

A woman can become pregnant only as long as an egg is in the **Fallopian tubes**. This knowledge can, of course, also be used to advantage by couples who want a child, and who can thus select an appropriate time for **coitus**. However, those who want to avoid a pregnancy only have to avoid coitus during the same period.

The fertile days of a woman are those shortly before, during, and after **ovulation**. It is advisable to begin periodical abstinence a few days before ovulation, because the sperm cells remain alive in the uterus and Fallopian tubes for several days. Abstinence for a while after ovulation is also necessary, because the egg can be fertilized for some time after ovulation.

There are basically two ways of determining the fertile days of a woman, namely, the "calendar method" and the "basal temperature method."

- The calendar method:
In order to use this method, the woman has to keep a careful record of her menstruations over a longer period of time (at least one year). Each period from the first day of menstruation to the day before the next menstruation counts as a separate **menstrual cycle**. After determining the various lengths of the individual cycles, one subtracts 17 days from the shortest cycle, and 13 days from the longest cycle. For example: Shortest cycle: 24 days; $24 - 17 = 7$. Longest cycle: 31 days; $31 - 13 = 18$. Now, if one counts again from each first day of menstruation, the fertile days are those between the 7th and 18th day of each cycle. The other days are infertile, that is, safe.

- The basal temperature method:
In order to use this method, the woman takes her own body temperature while resting. This is called the basal temperature. It has to be taken at the same time each day, for at least a year, and the findings have to be carefully recorded. Looking at the data for one month, the woman will notice an elevation of basal temperature during certain days. These

are her fertile days, since the rise in temperature results from her ovulation. By comparing the records of several months, the woman can then arrive at an estimate as to the periodical reoccurance of her fertile period.

Both the calendar method and the basal temperature method should not be used without professional guidance. Yet even under the supervision of a doctor, they are not very reliable. Particularly among younger women, menstrual cycles tend to be irregular. Ovulation can also occur at unexpected times due to emotional shock or illness. A rise in body temperature resulting from an infection can upset normal calculations. Finally, there is the possibility of ovulation in response to coitus itself. Apart from this lack of reliability, the rhythm method has another important disadvantage: it subjects sexual intercourse to the rule of calendar and thermometer and thus puts an emotional strain upon the sexual partners.

romance A romantic love affair.

The idea of romantic **love**, which was unknown to the ancient world, is a product of our Christian Western culture. It began to develop during the Middle Ages, when the notions of chivalry and religious devotion were, for the first time, applied to the courtly love that brave knights felt (or professed to feel) for their virtuous and largely inaccessible ladies. Indeed, the very notion of "courtship" has its origin in the **conventions** of a feudal court. However, the concept of romantic love did not necessarily imply sexual intercourse, and it also remained unrelated to the institution of marriage. It was not until the beginning of the industrial revolution and the period of Romanticism that the idea of romantic love as a condition for marriage became conceivable to a wider public. Thus, more and more people began to consider the selection of marriage partners as a matter of personal choice and, indeed, a personal right. At the same time, the traditional **family** structure also began to change. The former **extended family** was gradually replaced with the modern **nuclear family**, and today there is a widespread belief, particularly among young people, that there is only one "right" woman for every man, that their love should be romantic, and that it should lead to marriage. It should be pointed out, however, that neither happy love relationships nor happy marriages depend on such notions or conditions.

rubber A colloquial term for **condom**.

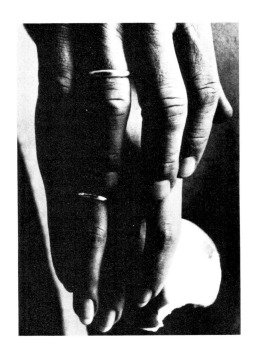

sadism Compulsion to hurt others in order to find sexual satisfaction. A sexual **perversion**.

sadist Term used to describe a man who finds pleasure in torturing others.

satisfaction The pleasurable experience of having a need fulfilled.

There are many different forms in which people can experience sexual satisfaction, although they usually involve the **genitals** and lead to **orgasm**. (See **coitus, masturbation, petting, sexual intercourse.**) In all of these cases, physical and psychological experiences are closely interrelated.

It should be remembered that sexual satisfaction is always satisfaction of a person as a whole, not just of his sexual urge. The sexual drive implies the need for personal contact, love, and tenderness.

Prolonged lack of sexual satisfaction usually creates problems. (See **abstinence.**)

scrotum The bag or pouch of skin which contains the **testicles** and which hangs between the thighs and behind the **penis**. The skin of the scrotum belongs to the **erogenous zones** and may be very sensitive to the touch.

seduction Seduction is often considered to be a dishonest and harmful act by which someone takes advantage of somebody else. (See **Don Juan.**) This view is clearly expressed in the legal definitions of seduction and related offenses. (See **sex legislation, statutory rape.**) However, under different circumstances, seduction can also be seen as something positive and advantageous for both partners, as for instance when they engage in flirting or in passionate courtship, or when marriage partners try to bring **variety** to their relationship. (See also **Casanova.**)

Many people dream of being seduced or being able to seduce others. Nevertheless, most of them also feel that, while among adults seduction may have its positive aspects, it cannot but be extremely harmful to **minors.** There is particular concern among many parents that their adolescent son or daughter might become a **homosexual** as a result of seduction by a homosexual adult or other adolescent. However, most scientific opinion today doubts this possibility. Isolated sexual acts do not seem likely to establish a permanent pattern of sexual behavior unless there is a definite predisposition which would manifest itself sooner or later even without premature encouragement. Furthermore, the great majority of reports by homosexuals themselves indicate that seduction has not been decisive in their development. (See also **homosexuality.**)

semen A thick, white liquid that is ejaculated from the penis during **orgasm.** It can contain up to 100 million sperm cells. The sheer quantity of semen is no indication of sexual **potency, masculinity,** or **fertility.** (See also **ejaculation.**)

sex appeal See **sexy**.

sex books
A colloquial term referring to books devoted to sexual matters. Such books may belong to the realm of literature such as novels (Petronius, "Satyricon"), poems (Ovid, "The Art of Love"), or plays (Aristophanes, "Lysistrata"). However, occasionally the term "sex book" is also applied to scholarly or scientific studies of human sexuality (Kinsey, "Sexual Behavior in the Human Male," or Masters/Johnson, "Human Sexual Response").

A classic example of erotic literature is the Indian "Kamasutra," which describes an elaborate system of rules for sexual intercourse, aimed at sexual refinement and a cultivation of the senses.

There are also many modern books (**sex manuals** or "marriage manuals") which provide detailed descriptions of different coital **positions**.

All of these books may be helpful in rediscovering the creative potential of human sexuality after a period of **prudery** and repression. However, it should be remembered that sexual problems usually have psychological causes and cannot therefore be solved by simply following pre-established patterns of behavior. Love is more than sexual technique. Even the best "sex book" can provide only a modest amount of secondary practical advice. The main source of sexual happiness is emotional maturity, or, in other words, a responsive and responsible attitude of the sexual partners towards each other.

Finally, it should also be mentioned that the term "sex book" is sometimes used for books which are exclusively aimed at sexual arousal.

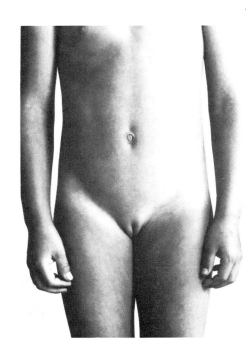

Such books (so-called "dirty books") provide the reader with a standard set of sexually stimulating images, and are, therefore, often used for the purpose of **masturbation**. There is no agreement among experts as to whether such books are harmful or beneficial. So far, there is not enough conclusive evidence to support either view. (See **pornography**.)

sex change See **transsexualism**.

sex drive

The human sex drive is already present in infancy and, like any other drive, it produces in the individual a state of tension that demands physical and psychological gratification. The way in which this gratification is obtained depends not only on biological, but also on cultural factors. (See **sexuality**.)

In small children, the sex drive is still unfocused and not yet centered on the **genitals**. During the several stages of a child's early **sexual development**, the tension caused by the drive is relieved first by oral, then by anal gratification until, eventually, genital gratification becomes the dominant outlet. In a mature person, the sex drive normally leads to **sexual intercourse** with others and may thus become a vehicle of procreation. However, the human sex drive is by no means restricted to this purpose. This is also evident from the fact that, in most cases, the sex drive remains undiminished after the **climacteric**, when reproduction has become impossible. It is obvious, therefore, that the human sex drive is not necessarily dependent on the presence of sex **hormones** in the body. (See also **castration**.)

sex education

Sex is an integral part of human life, and its significance can be fully understood only if it is related to the total human experience. Every individual's health and happiness, his sense of identity and self-esteem, his social adjustment and success very much depend, among other things, on the way in which he comes to terms with his **sexuality**. A proper sex education can help him to do so in a creative and constructive manner.

Unfortunately, many sex-education programs for young people rarely offer more than an explanation of the pertinent biological facts (**birth, pregnancy**) and the affirmation of certain cultural values (**abstinence, monogamy**). Such limited programs would be better described as "reproduction information" and "moral indoctrination." Nevertheless, even these timid and inadequate efforts have often been opposed by the public as going too far. Apparently, there are people who believe that, in the absence of formal instruction, no sex education takes place. This view is completely mistaken.

Every child is a sexual being from birth, and the denial, suppression, or rejection of his sexuality on the part of his parents and teachers cannot but affect the student's **sexual development**. In no case does sexual development result automatically in **maturity** and a full capacity to love. (See **perversion**.) On the contrary, every child's sexual growth is decisively influenced by the way his **father** and **mother** look at them-

161

selves and treat each other as sexual beings, how they react to questions about sex, and how they think and feel about other people. (See **Oedipus complex**.) Such sexual conditioning continues through **puberty**. Its effects can be positive or negative, but in any case they cannot be avoided. The choice is not between too much or too little, but only between good or bad sex education.

How can a good sex education be obtained?
There are still many people who believe that sex education is the exclusive responsibility of parents. These people overlook the fact that the modern world has become so complex that no two persons can offer an adequate preparation for it. Young people today are likely to encounter new situations for which their parents can find no parallels in their own experience.

The schools, on the other hand, are often hampered by the **prudery** of administrators and teachers, who are anxious to avoid any possible public criticism. Schools are social institutions and, as such, they reflect the fears and prejudices of society.

The churches undoubtedly have a vital role to play in the foundation of **sexual ethics**. However, they are only now beginning to overcome their traditional reluctance to discuss sex openly and to give their members some realistic instruction and positive guidance.

It should be obvious, therefore, that sex education is not a task for any one institution alone. Only the cooperation of all social agencies can provide young people with a comprehensive and balanced view of human sexuality. However, even the best public sex-education programs are confronted with some frustrating social realities:

- In our society, a young person reaches his sexual maturity in his early teens, but has to wait for his social maturity (legal adulthood) until the beginning of his twenties. (See **minor**.)

- The highly irrational character of most existing **sex legislation** undercuts the attempt to provide young people with sexual norms based on factual insight and the rule of reason.

- New, effective means of **birth control** have been developed, but continue to be largely unavailable to young, unmarried persons.

- Young people today may acquire a thorough theoretical knowledge of sex without being allowed to have any practical experience of it.

Under these circumstances, all sexual instruction must remain entirely abstract. The students are never permitted to exercise their sexual capacities, or to put the content of their lessons to any concrete test. They cannot prove themselves in actual situations with real sexual partners, accumulate and sort out their own sexual experiences, or learn by trial and error. In other words, sex education in the proper sense of the term is prohibited. All that can be hoped for is a sufficient amount of factual sex information coupled, perhaps, with some unofficial advice on how to find a workable compromise between private desire and public morality. These restrictions, which are imposed on no other educational discipline, give all official attempts at sex education a peculiar aura of unreality, if not insincerity, and undermine the credibility of even the most competent educator.

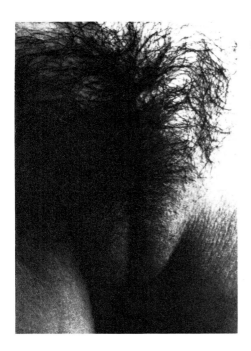

Eventually, this unfortunate handicap will be overcome only by a rigorous expansion of sex-education programs beyond the schools into all spheres of life:

- Colleges, universities, and other institutions of higher learning which train future professional and civic leaders must provide them with an adequate understanding of human sexuality and its vast social implications.

- Professional people such as doctors, teachers, ministers, lawyers, social workers, and police officers need special programs that discuss sexual behavior in its relation to particular professional issues.

- Adult sex-education programs must be greatly expanded. Sex education cannot stop after puberty, but has to continue through life. Adults need to keep up with advancing scientific knowledge to make their own sex lives more satisfying and to avoid a sexual "generation gap." Furthermore, there is an urgent need for an informed public opinion which will support reasonable changes in education and legislation.

- Finally, the mass media can greatly contribute to a more rational public approach to sex by avoiding sensationalism and the commercial exploitation of sex in favor of more extensive factual information.

These combined efforts may in time lead to the general realization that people of all ages, adults as well as adolescents and children, are sexual beings with sexual needs, and that the repression of these needs can only lead to **fear**, intolerance, injustice, misery, and disease.
On the other hand, the acceptance of sex as a creative force in human life can free people to engage in open dialogue, thus enabling them to develop genuine and satisfying solutions to their personal problems. This kind of mutual sex education by members of all age groups and cultural backgrounds will not only give everyone access to all sexual facts, but can also serve to bring about richer, happier sexual relationships and more meaningful lives. (See also **sexual revolution**.)

sexism An attitude or a philosophy that uses sexual differences as the basis of social discrimination. (See **double standard, matriarchy, patriarchy**.)

sex legislation Each state in the United States has its own laws regarding sexual behavior. These laws show an astonishing lack of conformity as to the number and character of punishable offenses as well as to the severity of the prescribed punishment. For example, certain sexual acts may be punishable by life imprisonment in one state, yet may not be a crime at all in another state. Furthermore, there is a total confusion as to the terminology used in defining sexual offenses. The various legal terms employed for this purpose are mostly of prescientific origin, and their meaning can differ from state to state. This extraordinary legal disparity and inconsistency make it impossible to describe the sex legislation of all 50 states accurately within the scope of the present volume.

163

However, one can recognize certain main areas of behavior that are subject to such legislation, and the legal attitudes towards them can briefly be summarized as follows:

■ Seduction:
Many states (although not all) have statutes that make it a crime to seduce a woman under a certain age by promising later marriage. In some states, the case can be dismissed if the marriage does indeed take place. The penalty for **seduction** can be as high as 10 years in prison and a fine of $5000.

■ Fornication:
The definitions of **fornication** vary from state to state. Generally, the term "fornication" is applied to sexual intercourse between unmarried persons. Some states have broadened this definition, others have narrowed it. The penalties range from a minimum of a $10 fine to a maximum of five years imprisonment plus a $5000 fine.

■ Adultery:
Adultery is sexual intercourse between partners of whom at least one is married to somebody else. Many states have statutes making adultery a crime. In some of these states, however, it is a crime only if committed repeatedly or openly. Penalties range from a $20 fine to five years imprisonment plus a $2000 fine.
Adultery statutes are today rarely enforced, as is evident in the State of New York, where until recently each year thousands of divorces were granted on grounds of adultery. Yet although adultery was also a crime there was never a conviction for adultery.

■ Incest:
Incest is illegal in all states of the union. However, some states differentiate between incestuous sexual intercourse and incestuous marriage, making the latter a lesser offense. The logic of this as of so many other sex laws is mysterious. The maximum penalty in any state for incest is 50 years imprisonment.

■ Rape:
Rape is sexual intercourse without a partner's lawful consent. Such lawful consent may be missing for a variety of reasons. For example, a woman may have been physically overpowered and forced to have sexual intercourse against her clear protest. However, she also may have consented under the threat of force, or because she was insane, or drunk, or deceived. In these and similar cases her consent would not have been lawful. Neither is a girl's consent lawful as long as she is under a certain age (18 years in most states). In this case, the crime committed against her is called **"statutory rape,"** and it is usually punished just as severely as all other kinds of rape. It does not make any difference whether the male involved was even younger than the girl or whether, in fact, she seduced him. The maximum penalty for rape is death or life imprisonment.
Because of the obvious injustices that can result from the rape statutes, many authorities have long recommended legal reform. However, so far little has been done to correct the situation.

164

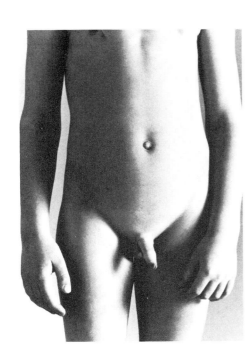

■ Prostitution:

Prostitution is illegal in all states of the union. Usually, the operators of **brothels**, procurers, and **pimps** are punished more severely than the **prostitutes** themselves, who often get away with a short jail sentence or a small fine. Some states have provisions for prosecuting the customer of a prostitute, and other states are able to do the same under some other general statute. However, prosecution of customers is extremely rare. This could be an expression of the sexual **double standard**.

■ Sodomy:

Many states have laws against acts of **"sodomy."** However, this term is so vague as to be practically meaningless. In some states it refers to **anal intercourse**. In others, it also includes **oral intercourse**. Sometimes it further includes mutual **masturbation, zoophilia**, and even necrophilia. It is obvious that such usage disregards all anthropological, medical, and psychological evidence that is available today. The anachronistic sodomy statutes mirror the prejudices and superstitions of former generations. Nevertheless, there have been few attempts to repeal them.

■ Crimes against Nature:

Some states also use the term **"crime against nature"** in referring to such varied sexual activities as **anal intercourse, cunnilingus, fellatio,** mutual **masturbation, pederasty,** and **zoophilia**. Occasionally, the terms "crime against nature" and "sodomy" are used interchangeably or side by side.

The term "crime against nature" is one of the most curious of legal terms, as it clearly implies that not any human being, but nature itself is the victim. However, the "nature" that the law endeavors to protect here is not the nature of natural science, but rather a mystical concept inaccessible to rational argument. In fact, modern scientific findings stand in sharp contrast to the archaic philosophy expressed in such legislation. As a consequence, most authorities on sexual matters today find themselves in a position where, for reasons of therapy, they counsel the public to engage in practices that are legally "against nature" and, therefore, crimes. The prescribed punishment for these crimes is often severe. The penalty can range up to a maximum of life imprisonment at hard labor.

The statutes covering "sodomy" and "crimes against nature," although applicable to everyone, including married couples, have usually been enforced only against male **homosexuals**. This is merely one, though hardly the only, illustration of the absurdity of such laws. (See also **unnatural sex**.) There have been repeated recommendations by legal authorities and by law-revision committees to abolish all laws against these so-called sexual "crimes without victims." Unfortunately, thus far progress in this area has been quite limited.

■ Obscenity:

There are innumerable statutes against obscenity. Such statutes can be concerned with obscene talk, obscene gestures, obscene material such as letters, books, pictures, films, and records, or generally "lewd and obscene behavior." Since there is no commonly accepted definition of what is obscene, these statutes are characterized by vagueness and obscurity. Their application is selective and unpredictable, and they are constantly being tested in the courts. On the whole, there seems to have been a liberalization in the last decade. Whether this trend will continue is open to question. (See **obscene, pornography.**)

Even a brief and superficial look at American sex legislation leads to the conclusion that it is, at best, a mixed blessing, the legacy of an unenlightened past, combining reasonable restrictions with unnecessary, unenforcable, petty regulations and uninformed narrow-minded moralizing. The main reason why such laws are still on the books is that they are rarely enforced, and thus most people are not aware of them. However, lack of enforcement is hardly the same as repeal. They can be enforced at any time against anyone who should displease the authorities, his business rivals, or his neighbors. There can be little doubt that the arbitrary and capricious character of many of these laws, together with their selective and haphazard enforcement, undermines the citizen's confidence in his ability to find justice and thus breeds disrespect for the entire legal system. (See also **sex offender.**)

sex manual

(also called "marriage manual") A book which attempts to teach married couples the elementary facts about **sexual intercourse,** and which usually also provides detailed descriptions of various coital **positions**.

In a period of inadequate **sex education,** such books were popular and indeed necessary, since even married couples were often quite ignorant in sexual matters. Unfortunately, such manuals often gave the false impression that sexual intercourse was a complicated technical process that could be mastered only with special skill and a great deal of expertise. This sometimes led certain people to the conclusion that true sexual **satisfaction** could only be achieved by means of sexual acrobatics. (See also **sex books**.)

sex offender

Someone who commits a sexual offense, or in other words a person whose behavior violates the criminal laws regulating sex.

Obviously, the concrete determination of what constitutes a sexual offense depends on the **sex legislation** of any given society. A society with few sex laws will have few sex offenders, while a society with extensive sex legislation is likely to have many. (It is, of course, another question whether such a society also enforces its laws. Without any change in actual human behavior, the number of known sex offenses in that society may rise or drop with stricter or more lenient enforcement.)

In the United States, each of the 50 states has its own sex legislation. Some sexual behavior may constitute a grave criminal offense in one state, yet may be perfectly legal in another state. Under these circumstances, it is impossible to give a comprehensive account of sexual offenses within the scope of the present volume.

Nevertheless, it is possible to point out certain sexual acts that are punishable in almost every society because they involve force or injury to other people. Such acts are characterized by the fact that they involve an identifiable victim who complains (or would complain if he could) to the authorities. Among such sexual offenses are abduction and **rape.** Some forms of **perversion,** such as sadism or pedophilia, may also cause considerable harm to other persons. Obviously, in these and similar cases, the public must be protected against the offender.

While no one disputes this necessity, there is some disagreement about the most effective way of obtaining such protection. Many authorities today believe that the imprisonment of sexual offenders without adequate medical treatment does more harm than good, as it eventually returns them unchanged into society, where they might commit new offenses. In cases where a perversion has led to the offense, professional treatment seems particularly important. Furthermore, since the clinical definition of a perversion implies a certain element of compulsion, the classification of an individual as a pervert also raises the question whether he is fully responsible for his actions. On the other hand, it seems defensible to demand that even perverts such as **exhibitionists** and **voyeurs** (peeping Toms), who are relatively harmless, should receive professional treatment in order to prevent them from becoming a public nuisance.

In addition to the type of offense just mentioned, there is a second group of sexual offenses that do not involve any victims, but consist of acts committed by consenting adults in private who have no intention of complaining to anyone. In the United States, such offenses may include **prostitution, oral** and **anal intercourse,** mutual **masturbation** (even between husband and wife), and sexual intercourse between unmarried partners, including **homosexual** partners. These so-called sexual "crimes without victims" would constitute the majority of known sexual offenses if the laws which prohibit them were constantly and equally enforced. However, it is quite obvious this cannot possibly be done. The laws are enforced only periodically and selectively against certain individuals or groups, thus creating a climate of injustice and hypocrisy. Such conditions in turn breed new crimes, such as blackmail and bribery. Unavoidably, they also lead to reprehensible police practices such as snooping and entrapment and to the corruption of law-enforcement officials.

It seems, therefore, that our society would greatly benefit from following the example of most other modern nations and the recommendations of such professional groups in this country as the American Law Institute, the Group for the Advancement of Psychiatry, and the National Commission on Reform of Federal Criminal Laws, by legalizing all sexual acts between consenting adults in private.

sex organs   See **genitals.**

sexual characteristics

The physical and psychological qualities that distinguish the sexes. (See also **body.**)

167

The primary sexual characteristics are the **genitals.**

The secondary sexual characteristics, which develop fully at **puberty,** are for males: facial **hair,** a protruding larynx (see **Adam's apple**), a deeper voice, and a stronger muscular development. For females: the **breasts,** softer hair, broader hips, and a generally weaker muscular development.

The tertiary sexual characteristics are certain psychological qualities normally attributed to one sex and discouraged in the other. These qualities are culturally determined and usually summarized in the concepts of **masculinity** and **femininity**. (See also **sexual roles.**)

sexual development

The eventual expression of the adult human **sex drive** not only depends on the maturation of the **body,** but is also shaped by a variety of educational and cultural influences.

In a small child, the sex drive is still diffuse. In infancy, the primary source of physical and emotional gratification is the mother. The satisfaction derived from this close relationship also encourages the infant to develop his abilities to touch and grab an object or person, stand up, walk, and speak. The confidence gained from his earliest experiences then enables him to turn to new, unfamiliar things and persons. He learns to distinguish between various objects, touches everything, takes everything apart. Beginning with his fourth year, he distinguishes the sexes. He experiences his first love for a person whom he now recognizes as belonging to the opposite sex. (See **Oedipus complex.**)

The child's own sexual identity is built up cumulatively through experience—through casual learning as well as explicit instruction. In short, a gender role is acquired in much the same way as a native language. Eventually, a child's sexual curiosity turns to his own and other people's **genitals.** He asks for their names and inquires about their functions. The reaction of parents and other adults to such questions and to his behavior in general greatly influences a child's development. Negative, hostile, or embarrassed reactions, a lack of parental love, persistent dishonesty or repression, can stunt a child's normal development and thus may result in a later **perversion.**

Early in his second decade, the child normally reaches **puberty.** The biological changes that take place inside the **body** at that time have their parallel in considerable emotional changes. The child not only matures physically but also begins to develop a sense of detachment from his parents and a growing need for independence.

His hitherto unconscious sexual drive turns towards persons of the other sex. This development, in order to lead to full **maturity,** needs explanations and encouragement on the part of adults. (See **adolescence, sex education.**)

sexual dream

Young people as well as adults may, on occasion, dream about sexual matters. Such dreams may be pleasant or unpleasant, familiar or strange and bizarre. However, their proper meaning can, if at all, be established only in the course of professional analysis by a psychoanalyst.

168

Young men may occasionally have an **ejaculation** in their sleep ("wet dream"), but it is also possible that girls experience **orgasm** while dreaming.

Sexual daydreams and fantasies are proof that our **sexuality** is an active force in our lives, even when we do not allow it full expression. Such daydreams do not mean that we are "dirty-minded" or sick, although, in some cases, they may reflect certain sexual **inhibitions** or even a **fear** of sex. In any event, these causes can be recognized and eliminated only by professional counselling.

sexual ethics

Throughout history, men have wrestled with the problem of sexual ethics or, in other words, with the question whether their own or other people's sexual behavior was good or bad. Today this question is as relevant as ever, although the answer has become more difficult than ever before.

All ethical standards are, of course, based upon certain fundamental beliefs, convictions, or assumptions, and the sexual ethics of any given culture reflect its assumptions about the purpose or "nature" of sex. For example, there have been peoples who were totally unaware of the causal connection between sex and procreation. Obviously, these peoples arrived at different standards for sexual behavior than those who believed that procreation was the only purpose of sex.

In our own culture, the latter belief was, for a very long time, shared by most people. The moral demands based on this belief were rarely questioned, because few individuals were ever exposed to other cultures with different value systems. On the contrary, in the closed societies of the past, customs and **conventions** were stable, and the universal acceptance of the same sexual morality could always be presumed. The common assumptions about the "nature" of sex seemed so obvious and self-evident to everyone that they did not have to be spelled out. (See **aberration, unnatural sex**.)

In the meantime, however, the explosive growth of the population, the advance of science and technology, and the increasing communication between different cultures have led to a re-examination of traditional beliefs and created a pluralism of values that was formerly unknown. We thus find ourselves today in a new historical situation. In the course of our lives, we encounter a great variety of conflicting opinions about the purpose of sex and are forced to choose between a number of competing value systems. (See **sexual revolution**.)

Although these systems differ in many important details, they can, for the purpose of clarification, perhaps be described as representing two basic types: the absolutistic and the relativistic moralities.

- The absolutistic or "old" morality is dogmatic and based on the belief demanded by the Holy Scriptures. Its highest value is compliance with the will of God. It can therefore also be described as a "morality of commandment." Those who obey the commandment are righteous; those who disobey thereby commit a **sin.** This morality assumes that that there is an eternal truth and that it is relevant for all times and for everyone under all circumstances.

169

- The relativistic or **"new morality,"** on the other hand, is rational and based on the knowledge gained by scientific research. Its highest value is human understanding, and it tries to judge each act individually according to time, place, and circumstances. It can therefore also be called "situation ethics." This is a "morality of consequences," which evaluates human behavior in the light of its effects on other human beings.

(Some people also distinguish a third type of sexual ethics: the hedonistic or "fun" morality, which holds that the highest value in life is pleasure. (See **hedonism**.) However, most hedonists will probably agree that pleasure is relative, that certain pleasures have to be avoided because of their unpleasant consequences, and that, eventually, only experience, understanding, and universal cooperation can lead the way to real happiness. In most respects, therefore, the hedonistic approach to moral questions is similar to the relativistic "morality of consequences.")

Within each of the two basic moral systems there is a variety of gradations. For example, even those who share the absolutistic approach of the "old morality" may arrive at quite different conclusions about certain concrete acts, because they disagree on the true "nature" of things or on the exact meaning of God's will. The adherents of the relativistic "new morality," on the other hand, may also disagree among themselves because they have different opinions about the consequences of certain acts, or because scientific knowledge in certain areas is still limited.

The struggle between the resulting different moralities has created the present moral confusion. However, today the "new morality" in one form or another seems to be gaining ground. It seems better suited to our fast-changing world, as it leaves more room for personal liberty and creativity. This does not necessarily mean that it demands less effort than the "old morality" which reduced all moral problems to the simple question of obedience. On the contrary, by making love and sex entirely a matter of human encounter and cooperation, the "new morality" encourages the individual to assume a greater share of responsibility towards his fellow men.

sexual intercourse
Physical contact with a sexual partner, leading to sexual **excitement** and **satisfaction.** More specifically: physical union between man and woman by inserting the **penis** into the **vagina.**

Sexual intercourse is the goal and most obvious expression of human **sexuality.** Male and female **genitals** complement each other. A woman's vagina is made to receive a man's penis. A man's penis, in a state of erection, can be inserted into the vagina. The physical movements of both penis and vagina during their sexual union can lead both sexual partners to the mutual stimulation of excitement to the point of **orgasm.**

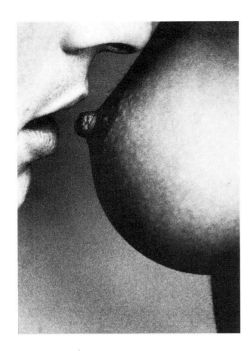

The physical union of penis and vagina is called **coitus.** It is usually considered to be the "normal" form of sexual intercourse, because it alone can result in pregnancy. Yet in most instances the sexual partners do not intend their sexual intercourse to lead to procreation. It is also true that men and women do not depend on coitus for their sexual satisfaction. They can be sexually excited and reach orgasm by various other forms of sexual contact. (See **anal intercourse, cunnilingus, fellatio, masturbation.**) It is therefore impossible to provide one single standard of sexual intercourse that could be valid for all people at all times.

The character of sexual intercourse is determined by several factors, of which the following are the most important: physical presence of a sexual partner, attitude of the sexual partners towards each other, stimulation and heightening of sexual excitement, and orgasm.

The physical presence of the sexual partner can be ascertained by looking at him, touching him, and by all other forms of sensory perception. The attitude of the sexual partners towards each other expresses itself in their active or passive reactions, their expectations, and their desire to please each other. The stimulation of sexual excitement can be achieved by any imaginable form of activity or passivity, as long as it contributes to mutual pleasure. This pleasure culminates in orgasm, which is then followed by a period of calm satisfaction. A man's orgasm, which is connected with his **ejaculation,** is usually followed by total relaxation. His inclination and his ability to continue sexual intercourse decrease. A woman, on the other hand, can have several orgasms within a matter of a few minutes. The female orgasm is connected with a number of physical reactions including vaginal and other muscular contractions. Many women have several orgasms before their male partner reaches his climax.

Sexual intercourse does not necessarily have to begin with **foreplay** or end with **coitus.** It is unreasonable to deride any sexual intercourse except coitus as "nothing but mutual masturbation." Coitus is only one of many forms of sexual intercourse. Some people experience more sexual excitement and pleasure by close embraces, or by reacting to certain movements or gestures, or sounds, or by encouraging their partners in certain actions, or by just submitting to their wishes. Everything that increases sexual excitement between two partners is part of sexual intercourse, whether it be different coital **positions** or any other type of variation. Sometimes even repetition can provide a special stimulus.

The experience of orgasm varies according to situation, mood, or form of sexual activity. At certain times, the experience is deeper than at others. An occasional failure to reach orgasm does not have to strain an otherwise happy sexual relationship. Simultaneous orgasm of both partners is either an agreeable coincidence or the result of a long-standing mutual adjustment. But even in this case, it should not be expected every time.

The basic premise for rewarding sexual intercourse is each partner's willingness to respect the other's wishes, hopes, and fears, and not to hurt his feelings. There are many people who want sexual intercourse only with a partner whom they can love. They need to combine sexual desire with affection, understanding, security, and trust. That can be true not only for couples who plan to marry, but also for more temporary relationships. For many people love and sex are inseparable. According to our official morality, sexual intercourse is allowed only within marriage. The relationship between sexual intercourse, emotional involvement, the institution of marriage, and procreation are viewed quite differently by different people. However, there can be no doubt that satisfying sexual relationships are also possible without strong emotional or institutional ties.

sexual intercourse during menstruation

In certain cultures women are considered "unclean" during **menstruation,** and they are therefore not allowed to have sexual intercourse at that time. However, there is no valid medical reason for this periodical abstinence. In fact, many women are particularly responsive just before or during their period.

Nevertheless, some couples may hesitate to have sexual intercourse during these days because of the bleeding. In such cases, the use of a **diaphragm** should be considered. It not only holds back the blood, but also acts as a means of **birth control.** This is important, since intercourse during menstruation can result in pregnancy. Depending on the timing of intercourse and the length of a woman's **menstrual cycle,** the male sperm cells may stay alive in her body until the next **ovulation.**

sexual intercourse during pregnancy

At the beginning of a **pregnancy,** a woman may, for a while, lose interest in sexual intercourse. Furthermore, as the pregnancy develops, her feelings during **coitus** may undergo some change. Nevertheless, sexual intercourse can continue, unless it causes pain or bleeding. However, it is obvious that the sexual partners should find a coital **position** which avoids pressure on the protruding abdomen. Various side positions seem to be appropriate for most couples.

During the last few weeks of a pregnancy, the contractions of the **uterus** during **orgasm** may initiate labor in some cases. A woman should therefore ask her physician for advice on this possibility. However, she should keep in mind that in such cases it does not make any difference whether the orgasm is caused by coitus or **masturbation.** All sexual intercourse should be stopped if the membranes are ruptured. This will reduce the chance of infection.

After a birth, it usually takes between 2 to 3 months before the female body is ready for another **conception.** However, sexual intercourse can be resumed as soon as the healing has progressed to the point that bleeding has ceased. Again, the exact timing and the appropriate technique of intercourse depend on the individual case and the advice of the doctor.

sexuality

In its broadest sense, sexuality can be understood as the psychic energy which finds physical and emotional expression in the **desire** for human contact, **tenderness, sexual pleasure,** and **love,** and which makes the **satisfaction** fo these basic needs possible.

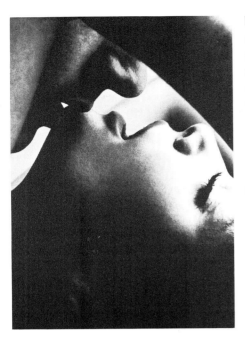

In professional language, sexuality is often referred to as an instinct or drive, that is, as an innate urge which creates a state of conscious and unconscious tension within the individual, and which compels him to seek appropriate gratification. The ways in which this gratification is obtained are dependent not only on biological, but also on cultural factors. (See **libido, sex drive, sexual development.**)

In the past, human sexual activity was always closely linked to the purpose of procreation. Even where reproduction was not the intended result of coitus, it could not be ruled out with certainty. Under these circumstances, most societies felt obliged to subject the sexual activity of their members to considerable restrictions. (See **abstinence, conventions, sex legislation, taboo.**) However, sexuality is an integral part of human life that cannot be manipulated or suppressed at will. (See also **monogamy.**) Today, for the first time in history, progress in the area of **birth control** enables mankind to break the traditional link between sex and procreation. The implications of this development have not yet been fully understood. (See **sexual revolution.**)

sexual pleasure

Pleasure is the strongest motive for sexual activity. Sexual interest and **excitement** find their obvious goal in the most intense physical pleasure: **orgasm.** However, already the increase of excitement before orgasm is experienced as pleasure. It is characteristic of the sexual drive that the desire as well as its fulfillment create pleasurable feelings.

The ability to experience pleasure does not develop spontaneously, but has to be acquired. Each man and each woman needs time to understand his or her own capacities for pleasure. The understanding of this capacity, its affirmation, and its expression grow out of personal encounters with a sexual partner. It is therefore very difficult to give a theoretical description of sexual pleasure. This is one reason why sex educators often avoid discussing it. However, it is even more difficult to provide an adequate picture of human sexuality without mentioning sexual pleasure. It is an important part of the capacity for personal contact and **love.** The chronic inability to experience sexual pleasure is a symptom of an emotional disorder.

Everything that brings mutual pleasure strengthens a sexual relationship. However, one can encounter divergent opinions as to the nature and value of sexual pleasure. For instance, many people believed in the past that it was unbecoming for a woman to experience and express sexual pleasure. Even today, sexual pleasure is often discouraged or looked upon with suspicion. There are people who still demand that sexual pleasure should always be tied to the purpose of procreation. They view with apprehension any attempt to heighten sexual pleasure by a **variety** of sexual practices and different coital **positions.** Still other people argue against sexual pleasure because they believe it to lead to a sexual consumer mentality, eroding mutual respect and concern between sexual partners. However, such fears seem hardly justified. There are probably more unhappy men and women who find too little sexual pleasure in their lives than there are people who suffer from over-indulgence. (See also **hedonism.**)

sexual revolution

The term "sexual revolution" is an attempt to describe the fact that during the last decades the problems connected with human **sexuality** have acquired a new meaning.

While the actual sexual behavior of most people has changed less than it might seem, the motivations, implications, and consequences of this behavior have changed a great deal. In other words, the same sexual acts now occur under entirely new conditions, and within a different context.

This context is, of course, man-made. As man has learned to control nature, he has, at the same time, created a new social environment for himself, a new historical situation with new, unprecedented problems demanding new, unprecedented solutions. It is becoming increasingly obvious that the time-honored models and old approaches no longer work. A transvaluation of values seems unavoidable.

A symptom of this development is the dispute over the importance and the virtues of **sex education.** According to the traditional concept of sexuality, sex education was superfluous. There were only a few known biological facts and a few simple, unalterable moral principles which were handed down from one generation to the next without questioning. As there was little change in the external circumstances of life, and as contact with other cultures and different value-systems was limited, the experiences of older people remained valid for their children and grand-children. In the meantime, however, technological progress has changed the world to such an extent that previous human experiences are becoming irrelevant. The young and the old, the married as well as the unmarried, find themselves confronted with a totally new situation. There is, therefore, a continuous public and private discussion of sex, not because it is fashionable, but because it is indispensable. There is a need for new attitudes which can help us cope with present and future developments. In order to form such an attitude towards sex, we have to examine it in all of its aspects. It is for this reason that our sexual values can no longer be found in unquestioned traditions, but have to be newly determined on the basis of our continually increasing scientific knowledge. However, because of its very increase, such knowledge is subject to constant revision. It is obvious, therefore, that modern sex education cannot afford to be dogmatic. In discussing sexual problems, it can and must try to present the available facts, but it cannot impose the solutions. There are several areas where new solutions have to be found:

- The traditional sexual values were patriarchal. (See **double standard, patriarchy, woman.**) Today we need new approaches that can lead us towards true sexual partnership between men and women. However, we do not know in advance what these approaches should be, and what true **equality of the sexes** will bring about in tomorrow's society.
- Because of the threat of overpopulation, and since new, effective methods of **birth control** have been found, sex can no longer be restricted to the purpose of procreation. The eventual effects of this development are still largely unpredictable. However, it is already apparent that sexual intercourse as such has gained an importance of

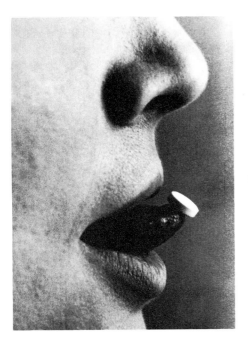

its own as a means of personal communication. It can be a mere source of pleasure as well as the appropriate expression of a deep human relationship. Thus the founding of a **family** is no longer the sole purpose of **marriage.** Two people may marry, not because they want children, but because they want to share their lives with each other. On the other hand, sexual activity can no longer remain the privilege of the married. Neither does the sexual behavior of adolescents or single adults have to follow the pattern of marital sex.

■ Since, in the past, sexuality was tied to procreation, the only "right" sexual activity was **genital intercourse.** Consequently, every sexual act other than **coitus** was considered "perverse" or an **aberration.** Today a sexual relationship tends to involve each partner as a whole person, not just his genitals. The demand to restrict sexual contact to particular areas of the body is therefore unreasonable and, in itself, perverse. **Oral** and **anal intercourse** can be appropriate forms of sexual activity. Laws and statutes aimed at preventing such activity are obsolete and need to be changed. (See **sex legislation.**)

■ In the past, **sexuality** was believed to be a single, isolated, controllable force which appeared during **puberty,** and which was to be employed only after the wedding. Before marriage, or outside of it, **abstinence** was the only accepted behavior. Today we know that sexuality is an integral part of every human life from its beginning, and that our character as adult human beings is the result of a long and complicated **sexual development.** This new knowledge has important consequences for our moral attitudes.

All of these fundamental changes give us a new sense of freedom. The traditional rules and regulations are becoming meaningless; their continued enforcement is irrational and repressive. Sexual repression is the main tool of dictatorships, because it creates a climate of hate and fear which can be exploited for the preservation of power. A democracy, on the other hand, is based on equality, mutual trust, and cooperation. The trend towards such cooperation is world-wide. Changes in the sphere of sex mirror the greater changes that are taking place in human society.

Everywhere privileges are being abolished, power has to be shared, and there is a constantly growing demand for democratic participation. However, in a democracy life is not necessarily easier or more comfortable than in a dictatorship. Often it is more complicated and even more frustrating. The old, dictatorial morality repressed sexuality and individual freedom. It gave the appearance of law and order. The **new morality** is more difficult. It makes greater demands on the individual and forces him to take on new responsibilities.

In our society today, both the old and the new morality exist side by side. The resulting moral confusion can be overcome only by increased understanding, tolerance, and patience.

175

sexual roles

In all societies the obvious biological difference between men and women is used as a justification for forcing them into different social roles which limit and shape the expression of their **sexuality.** The resulting difference in sexual behavior is then taken as a further manifestation of biological differences which confirm the need for different social roles.

Although this kind of circular logic proves nothing beyond its own assumptions, it is socially very effective. For example:

Our own society, which still has the character of a **patriarchy,** encourages every **man** to assume a socially dominant position and to prove his fitness to do so by displaying the signs of **masculinity.** A **woman,** on the other hand, is expected to signalize her acceptance of a secondary social position by cultivating her **femininity.** The **male** social role is designed to reward masculine men, while the **female** social role offers its relative advantages only to feminine women. (The aggressive man will run the bigger business; the pretty, agreeable girl will find the richer husband.) In other words, masculinity and femininity are sexual values which are developed in response to social inequality. However, once they have been developed, they justify and cement it. The social and sexual roles of men and women mutually reinforce each other.

Obviously, this psychological mechanism can operate only as long as the sexuality of men and women does not transgress the limits set by their social roles. Every society tries, therefore, to prevent such transgressions by calling the socially defined sexual roles "natural," eternal, and unchangeable. Any person who refuses to accept them is prosecuted as a **deviant** and punished as an offender not only against society, but against "nature" itself. A historical example of such deviance is the case of Joan of Arc who, as a young girl, not only led the French army to victory over the English, but also wore a male battledress. In her later trial she was promptly accused of having thereby violated the laws of nature. (See also **crime against nature, unnatural sex.**)

Over the centuries, many people have, of course, wondered why allegedly "natural" roles should need such rigorous social enforcement. After all, if they were truly natural, they would "come naturally" to both men and women. However, it is noteworthy that the advocates of the so-called "natural" inequality of the sexes resent nothing more than letting "nature" take its course. Nevertheless, if their arguments were true, there would be no need to deny women equal opportunities, since they would be unable to compete with men. If women were "naturally" inferior, men would have nothing to fear. However, the fact that many men do fear such competition raises sufficient doubt as to the validity of their arguments.

The truth is that human sexual desires and capacities have a tendency to go beyond the narrow limits of any social role. Indeed, it takes a constant, combined effort by all social authorities to keep this tendency under control. Such social control appears not only externally, in the form of parental guidance, peer-group pressure, and law enforcement, but also internally in the form of concepts and values which determine the self-image of every individual, and it is in the individual mind where the confusion of sexual identity and social role can create the most serious problems.

For example, since men have been told that women are socially and sexually passive, they are usually gravely disturbed by encountering a woman who is socially aggressive, and who takes the initiative in sexual intercourse. Confronted with this "lack of femininity" in a woman, a man may feel tempted to dispute her womanhood. If this contention does not hold up in face of the evidence, he may instead begin to doubt his own **virility** and become impotent.

However, the confusion goes still further. The notion that in every sexual encounter there has to be one active (masculine) and one passive (feminine) partner is so persistent that it not only ruins many heterosexual relationships, but also influences the behavior of certain homosexuals who feel compelled to model themselves after these stereotypes. By doing so, they give support to the curious belief that even in sexual relationships between members of the same sex, there always has to be one to play the "male" role, while the other must assume that of the "female." There is, in fact, a general impression that every homosexual couple (whether male or female) consists of one active, masculine and one passive, feminine partner. People who hold this belief are, of course, at a total loss to explain phenomena like the famous homosexual elite troups of ancient Greece, which consisted entirely of male lovers.

All of these views are based on a wrong conclusion drawn from a false assumption. The false assumption states that women are naturally passive, while men are naturally active. The wrong conclusion asserts that every passive person is playing a female role and that every active person plays the role of a male.

These misconceptions stand in the way of true sexual equality. They prevent many men from accepting women as full partners. The **emancipation** of women will not be complete until it becomes conceivable to both sexes that active and passive attitudes can be appropriate for either of them, and that even two "active" partners can have a rewarding relationship.

The fact of the matter is that activity and passivity have nothing to do with the biological difference between the sexes. The sexual roles of men and women can and do change with their social roles. The best way to prevent confusion in this area is by creating true social and sexual equality, and by making the social and sexual roles flexible enough to allow for an unfettered development of all human sexual capacities. (See also **conventions, equality of the sexes.**)

sexual union   See **coitus, sexual intercourse.**

sexy   Sexually attractive.

Men and women try to become more attractive to potential sexual partners through their dress, hair-styles, colognes or perfumes, and by moving or speaking in a certain manner. This does not necessarily mean an invitation to sexual intercourse. The sexual attractiveness of a woman depends, to a large extent, on the man's ability to react to her. No woman can be attractive to all men, since not all men respond to the same stimuli. Neither are all women attracted to the same masculine traits. To a considerable degree, "sex appeal" is a matter of taste, changing life-styles, and fashions.

SIECUS

These initials stand for "Sex Information and Education Council of the U.S."

SIECUS is a voluntary non-profit health organization, dedicated to the establishment and exchange of information and education about human sexual behavior. It tries "to establish man's sexuality as a health entity: to identify the special characteristics that distinguish it from, yet relate it to, human reproduction; to dignify it by openness of approach, study, and scientific research designed to lead toward its understanding and its freedom from exploitation; to give leadership to professionals and to society, to the end that human beings may be aided toward responsible use of the sexual faculty and toward assimilation of sex into their individual life patterns as a creative and re-creative force."

In conjunction with these efforts, SIECUS has published a number of books, pamphlets, and study guides related to problems of human sexuality. SIECUS also supports a nationwide program of **sex education.** The SIECUS national headquarters is located in New York City.

sin

A religious term referring to an act or a state of existence that is contrary to the will of God.

Theologians often prefer to use the word "sin" in the singular, implying that it is, above all, a negative attitude towards God and one's fellow man. The individual actions resulting from this attitude are then called "sins." Laymen normally use this plural, as they are generally more concerned with the acts themselves than with their motivation.

According to this common usage, everything that violates social **conventions** or regulations can be called a "sin." Thus, at one time, the entire sphere of human **sexuality** came to be considered as sinful. Sexual **desire, masturbation, premarital intercourse,** and **homosexual** behavior were believed to be sinful in themselves, because all of these things were feared by a prudish society. However, such a belief can only lead to more fear and, eventually, to a condemnation of life itself.

It is for this reason that many theologians today urge a return to the examination of attitudes. For it is the basic attitude of men towards each other that determines the moral value of their actions. The negative attitude, the true sin against God and one's neighbor, is characterized by a lack of love. Whether sex is sinful or not is therefore determined by the love that people give or deny to each other. (See **new morality.**)

single

A term used for adults who are not part of a married couple.

There was a time when men were not allowed to marry unless they fulfilled certain requirements, such as full qualification in their trade or profession, and the proven ability to support a family. Women, on the other hand, remained unmarried when nobody courted them. Since the unmarried status thus resulted from social customs and regulations, it was considered something necessary and inescapable. The unmarried individual had no choice but to adjust to a single way of life. However, this adjustment was normally helped by the fact that the **extended family** had room for married couples of several generations as well as for a number of unmarried relatives.

Today more people get married than ever before. According to the now prevailing opinion, a single person has quite voluntarily chosen his way of life because he did not want to get married. It is also generally expected that single men and women practice sexual **abstinence,** because they might choose their sexual partners from among those already married. This is also the reason why single persons, particularly single women, often meet with suspicion on the part of married couples. In contrast to men, women are also publicly identified as unmarried by being addressed as Miss instead of Mrs. Furthermore, the social status of married women is usually higher than that of single women, although the latter are often better informed and take a more active part in cultural and political affairs.

The future is likely to bring the full social equality of all women, regardless of their marital status. This equality will also mean increased possibilities for social contact between men and women, and an equal right to sexual activity.

sissy

A derogatory slang expression referring to a boy or a man who fails to display the expected signs of **masculinity**.
Since the concept of masculinity is subject to change, the concrete meaning and the effect of the word "sissy" depend very much on the cultural context in which it is used. (See also **sexual roles.**)

sixty-nine

Slang term used to describe a form of **oral intercourse** in which the sexual partners simultaneously lick each other's genitals. (See **cunnilingus, fellatio.**) In doing so, the position of their bodies in relation to each other is similar to that of the inverted numerals in the number 69.

sodomy

A term formerly used for **anal intercourse** (with men, women, or animals).

The word is derived from the biblical city of Sodom, which was destroyed by God. According to some traditional interpretations (which are now disputed), the people of Sodom engaged in anal intercourse, and were punished by God for this reason. However that may be, the terms "sodomite," "sodomy," and "to sodomize" generally were used to express disgust at unfamiliar sexual practices. The exact meaning of these words varied accordingly. Often they were used in the same indiscriminate way as **"perversion."** Because of its unscientific character, the term "sodomy" is now becoming obsolete. (See also **sex legislation.**)

spermatic duct

(Latin: "vas deferens") The male body contains two spermatic ducts which carry the **spermatozoa** from the **testicles** to the **urethra,** which, in men, serves for the discharge of both urine and **semen.**
The cutting and tying of the spermatic ducts for the purpose of **sterilization** is called **vasectomy.**

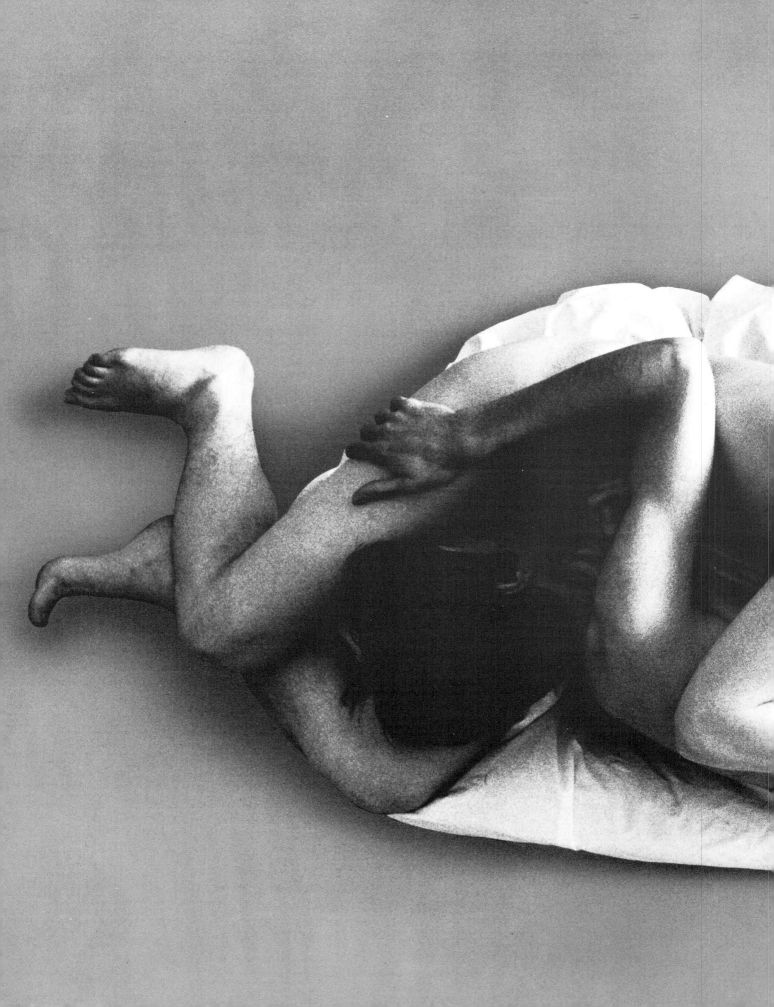

spermatozoa

(singular: spermatozoon) Sperm cells. Male reproductive cells which are produced in the **testicles.** A spermatozoon has a length of about 1/600 of an inch, and it consists of a short oval head and a long tail which, by its movements, allows the cell to travel through the **vagina** into the **uterus.** Spermatozoa can remain fertile inside a woman's body up to several days after **ejaculation.**

spermicides

Vaginal spermicides are available in different forms, such as jellies, creams, aerosol foams, foaming tablets, and suppositories. They are used for the purpose of **birth control,** sometimes in combination with a **diaphragm** or a **condom.**

Before intercourse, the spermicidal preparations are inserted into the **vagina,** where the chemicals contained in them kill the sperm and thus prevent pregnancy. If, for some reason, the spermicide fails, and pregnancy does occur, the baby will in no way be affected.
Spermicidal products are available in drugstores without prescription. However, in order to increase their effectiveness, women should ask a doctor for instructions as to their proper use and follow them carefully. (See also **reliability of birth control methods.**)

statutory rape

A legal term referring to cases where a partner's consent to engage in sexual intercourse, although clearly expressed, is not lawful. (See **sex legislation.**)

sterility

See **infertility.**

sterilization

A man or a woman who does not want any more children may decide to undergo minor surgery resulting in **infertility.** Such voluntary sterilization is called **vasectomy** in the case of men, and **tubal ligation** in the case of women. Both operations are safe and simple, but irreversible. They do not affect the sexual capacities.
Voluntary sterilization is legal in all 50 states.

streetwalker

Slang term for a female **prostitute.**

strip-tease

Striptease dancers are girls who professionally remove their clothing in front of an audience according to certain techniques calculated to create suspense and excitement in the spectator. Such performances take place in theatres (burlesque), as well as in bars and nightclubs.
Striptease combines elements of show business with sexual stimulation. It offers performers and spectators an opportunity to express tendencies towards exhibitionism and voyeurism that must be suppressed in everyday life. It can be argued, therefore, that striptease serves a social purpose, although it may not be to everybody's taste. (See also **go-go girl.**)

stud

A slang term for a sexually very active man or one who sells his sexual services to women. (See **prostitution.**)

sublimation

A psychoanalytic term referring to a highly complex process in which erotic energy is channelled into various non-sexual activities. (See also **libido.**)

Among laymen, the concept of "sublimation" is often misunderstood and misapplied. There is a popular notion that a man could easily control, suppress, or even eliminate his sexual desires by exhausting his strength in physical work, sports, or increased intellectual effort, or by devoting his whole attention to helping others. This is a total misconception. People who act on this erroneous assumption are bound to be disappointed. The term "sublimation" is out of place where practical educational problems are concerned.

swinger

A slang expression meaning a person who leads a life of sexual **promiscuity.** (See also **group sex.**)

symptoms of pregnancy

A woman usually suspects being pregnant if she misses a **period** after having had **sexual intercourse.** However, the absence of an expected **menstruation** is not necessarily conclusive evidence of a **pregnancy.** Further possible symptoms are a feeling of nausea, particularly in the morning ("morning sickness"), an increased tenderness and a swelling of the breasts, an increased need to urinate, certain discolorations of the skin (resembling large freckles), and after some time, a weight gain and the enlargement of the abdomen.

Most women are, of course, interested in learning about their pregnancy as soon as possible. Certain pregnancy tests, which are conducted in a laboratory, can provide relatively quick answers. The most commonly used is the urine test, which takes only a few minutes, and which will prove positive, that is, indicate a pregnancy, if the urine contains a certain hormone called "chorionic gonadotropin." However, although the urine test is fairly accurate, neither a positive nor a negative result is necessarily 100% reliable.
A reliable symptom of pregnancy is provided by the movements of the **fetus** inside the mother's womb, which can be felt after the 4th month of pregnancy. An infallible sign of pregnancy is the heartbeat of the fetus, which can be heard by an examining physician. (See also **unwanted pregnancy.**)

syphilis

(or lues) One of the **venereal diseases.**

Syphilis is almost always contracted through **sexual intercourse** with an infected partner. Only in very rare instances is the disease transmitted through contaminated objects, such as towels or toilet seats. Syphilis can also be transmited from an infected mother to her unborn child.

187

Syphilis is caused by a micro-organism called spirocheta pallida, which enters the body through a lesion in the skin. Some time afterwards, a small ulcer develops at the spot where the germ entered, usually in the genital area. This ulcer, which normally appears about 3 weeks after infection, is small, hard, and painless. (In some cases, a woman may not even notice it.)

At this first stage, the disease is still easily curable. However, the ulcer disappears after a while even without treatment, which can lead the patient to the false impression that he is cured. In actual fact, the disease has now entered its second stage, which soon manifests itself in a rash on part or all over the body. Both this rash and the initial ulcer are highly infectious. Again the symptoms disappear even without treatment, and the disease now enters its third stage. The syphilis germs withdraw from the skin to the inside of the body where, many years later, they may attack the liver, the heart, or the brain, causing paralysis and death.

It should be obvious from this brief sketch that syphilis is a very dangerous disease which requires the earliest possible treatment. Given this early treatment, syphilis can fairly easily be cured. The presence or absence of syphilis in a patient is established by means of a blood test (Wassermann test).

taboo Originally, a Polynesian term referring to somebody or something that is forbidden or sacred. In the meantime, the word "taboo" has entered the vocabulary of most modern languages, and today it is usually applied to persons, things, or actions that are considered too dangerous or disturbing to talk or even think about. The violation of a taboo is always punished, either directly and officially by law, or indirectly by a variety of private social sanctions.

Every society has its own religious, legal, social, political, and sexual taboos, although their number and character may change in the course of time. However, it is always characteristic of a taboo that no reason or justification for its existence is provided. Indeed, a taboo may very well be defined as an unexplained prohibition. In fact, the demand for an explanation is, in itself, already a violation of the taboo.

It is quite obvious that the existence of taboos poses a challenge to the spirit of scientific inquiry. The very concept of science, the desire to question and understand everything, implies the investigation and eventual elimination of taboos. However, the elimination of all taboos does not necessarily mean the abolition of all prohibitions. On the contrary, wherever such prohibitions can be shown to have a rational justification, they will be confirmed and strengthened by the findings of science. These reasonable prohibitions, however, would no longer have the character of taboos.

One of the oldest sexual taboos of mankind is the incest taboo or, in other words, the prohibition against having sexual intercourse with close relatives. Throughout history, this taboo has been almost universally accepted, and it still is effective today. (See **incest.**) However, certain other traditional taboos, such as that against **sexual intercourse during menstruation,** have lost their former importance. On the other hand, modern civilization has created a number of new sexual taboos which would have been incomprehensible to the ancient world. An example is the taboo against sexual intercourse (outside of marriage) with even a sexually mature **minor.** Another manifestation of a modern sexual taboo is the existence of euphemisms for sexual acts or objects and the prohibition against so-called "four-letter words." (See also **Glossary of Sexual Slang** at the end of the book.) Still another example is the widespread aversion to acknowledging the existence of so-called illegitimate sexual practices. (See **monogamy.**)

The only way in which we can liberate ourselves from the tyranny of taboos is not by blindly breaking them, but by trying to find the possible reason behind them and to understand their importance and meaning for other people. At the same time, we should also question our own motives and preconceptions. Such a rational approach to the problem of taboos can lead us to a realistic attitude and a responsible course of action.

tampon   A roll of cotton or similar absorbent material which is introduced into the **vagina** in order to absorb the menstrual flow. (See **menstruation.**)

Compared to sanitary pads, tampons have the advantage of being undetectable even under tight-fitting clothes. As long as tampons are replaced often enough, there is no medical objection to their use. However, in cases of heavier menstrual bleeding, they are less appropriate.

tenderness   The physical expression of appreciation and **love** is essential in every sexual relationship. The need for tenderness, for affectionate bodily contact, is one of the most fundamental human needs. Tenderness is one of the most important means of creating and conveying a sense of acceptance.

True tenderness is always a sign of respect and concern. The most intense kind of tenderness possible between human beings is **sexual intercourse.**

testicles   Male sex glands. Two ovoid bodies contained in the **scrotum** which produce sex **hormones** and **spermatozoa.**
A man's testicles correspond in their function to a woman's **ovaries.**
The loss or removal of one testicle does not eliminate sexual **potency.**

transsexual   A person who wants to be a member of the opposite sex. A transsexual is a man who wants to be a woman, or a woman who wants to be a man.

transsexualism   is the term used to describe the tendency of some people to have their sex changed. Modern surgical techniques have made such operations possible in a certain number of cases.

It is a matter of further definition whether the terms "transsexualism" and "sex change" are also appropriate in connection with **hermaphrodites** who undergo medical treatment in order to find a distinct sexual identity. Except for some extremely rare cases, a person's sex can be clearly identified by examining the cells of his body. Still, the formation of his

genitals may be far less conclusive. In such cases, hormonal and surgical treatment can succeed in establishing a definite male or female physical identity. However, it is also possible that persons whose sex is clearly not in doubt express the wish for a sex change. These people are bound to encounter considerable personal difficulties. **Masculinity** and **femininity,** and the ability to accept gender roles, are determined more by educational and social influences than by biological factors. Consequently, hormone injections and surgery alone cannot bring about a genuine sex change. These measures have to be augmented by an extensive psychological treatment. (See also **sexual roles.**)

It is obvious that such a highly complicated venture as a sex change can be undertaken only after careful professional counselling.

transvestite

A person who disguises himself as a member of the opposite sex and wants to be treated accordingly.

People who, for their sexual satisfaction, totally depend on this disguise suffer from transvestism, a sexual **perversion.** However, since the **sexual roles** in our culture can prove too rigid and restrictive for many people, the mere fact that somebody enjoys wearing clothes of the opposite sex does not, in itself, make him a pervert. Neither is a transvestite necessarily a **homosexual.** (See also **masculinity.**)

tubal ligation

Female **sterilization** operation, consisting of the tying and cutting of the **Fallopian tubes,** thus blocking the passage of the ovum (egg) into the womb. This operation results in the woman's **infertility,** but does not, in any way, diminish the sexual capacities.

Tubal ligation is just as safe and effective as **vasectomy,** but somewhat more complicated to perform. The result should be considered final. The operation is legal in all 50 states.

twins

Two children of one mother who are born as a result of the same **pregnancy.**

There are two kinds of twins: those born from one egg (identical or monozygotic twins) and those born from two eggs (fraternal or dizygotic twins). (See **zygote.**)

In the case of identical twins the fertilized egg divides into two separate parts and each of these develops into an **embryo.** Identical twins are always of the same sex and resemble each other closely.

Fraternal twins, on the other hand, may resemble each other no more than other brothers and sisters. Although a woman's **ovaries** usually release only one egg (**ovum**) during a menstrual cycle, occasionally two or more eggs may be released and fertilized by different **spermatozoa.** In these cases, the birth of fraternal twins, triplets, quadruplets, or so on may result.

During the pregnancy itself, it is difficult to determine with certainty whether a woman is expecting a multiple birth. (X-ray examinations, which could provide the information, are better avoided.)

Twins, triplets, quadruplets, and other such sets are usually born somewhat earlier than other children.

unnatural sex

An old-fashioned term intended to express disapproval of certain sexual practices.

Depending on the culture and the historical period in which the term was used, it could refer to anything from masturbation to the most unusual forms of perversion. In other words, the meaning of the term has changed so often that it is impossible to provide an objective, clear, and lasting definition for it. However, this lack of definite meaning has, if anything, made the term even more popular. The underlying psychological mechanism operating here is easily explained:

People generally have a tendency to attribute objective value to their subjective tastes and opinions. They are apt to confound their personal concepts of reality with reality itself, and therefore call "natural" everything that they believe to be "right." This kind of argument seems particularly attractive to people who want to protect their privileges or unreasonable policies. Thus at one time monarchy was declared to be the only "natural" form of government, the institution of slavery was explained as representing the "natural" order of things, and women were considered to be "naturally" inferior to men. Although such pseudo-justifications have long been rejected in most social areas, they somehow still seem to work in the sphere of sex.

For example, a person who considers procreation as the only justification for sexual activity is unlikely to be content stating this moral conviction but rather will insist that, quite apart from his personal views, it is the "nature" of sex to result in pregnancy, and that all sexual behavior that cannot lead to that goal is "unnatural." This then includes **masturbation, homosexual** acts, **coitus interruptus,** and all other forms of **birth control.**

On the other hand, there are people who believe that it is the "nature" of sex to create a life-long bond of affection between two persons of different sex. Accordingly, even **anal** and **oral intercourse,** although

192

neither can result in pregnancy, are considered "natural" as long as they occur between **heterosexual** couples. However, the same acts between homosexual couples would still be described as "unnatural."

There are still others who maintain that it is the true "nature" of sex to provide pleasure and personal contact between people, regardless of sex or age. Consequently, for them everything is "natural" as long as it is enjoyable.

Finally, there are those neutral observers for whom nothing can possibly be "unnatural," since everything occurs within nature. For them, pain is just as natural as pleasure, disease just as natural as health, and death just as natural as life. In short, the only unnatural thing is one that does not exist, and the only unnatural act is one that cannot be performed. Obviously, it is only this latter, scientific approach that uses the words "natural" and "unnatural" as purely descriptive terms. However, it is equally obvious that, as such, they are practically meaningless. Scientists therefore do not use such terms, but relegate them to the sphere of morals.

As this brief summary indicates, the term "unnatural" is a value judgment, not a statement of any fact or actually existing condition. However, since this value judgment appears, as it were, under a false label, disguised as an objective truth, it can easily lead to confusion and is, therefore, unsuitable for any rational discussion. (See also **aberration, crime against nature, perversion.**)

unwanted pregnancy

An unwanted pregnancy usually creates problems for which no easy answers are possible.

Obviously, the prevention of a pregnancy by means of **birth control** is always preferable to an **abortion.** Thus an unwed mother who is opposed to having an abortion may rather prefer to put her unwanted baby up for adoption. Others may eventually accept their child, and even develop a special love for it. However, if a woman decides to have an abortion, she should not look for a criminal abortionist, but try to obtain a legal, safe, and medically competent abortion in a regular hospital or in a doctor's office. Since many of the 50 states have liberalized their abortion laws, legal abortions are now within reach of virtually every American woman. In most major American cities, the Planned Parenthood offices will provide the necessary assistance. If no local help is available, information and referral will be provided by Planned Parenthood-World Population, 810 Seventh Avenue, New York, New York 10019, Telephone: (212) 541–7800.

urethra

Urinary duct. The duct through which urine is released. In men, the urethra also serves for the **ejaculation** of **semen,** and, beginning at the bladder, it runs through the **penis,** ending at the tip of the **glans.** In women, the external opening of the urethra lies between the **clitoris** and the opening of the **vagina,** and it serves exclusively for the release of urine.

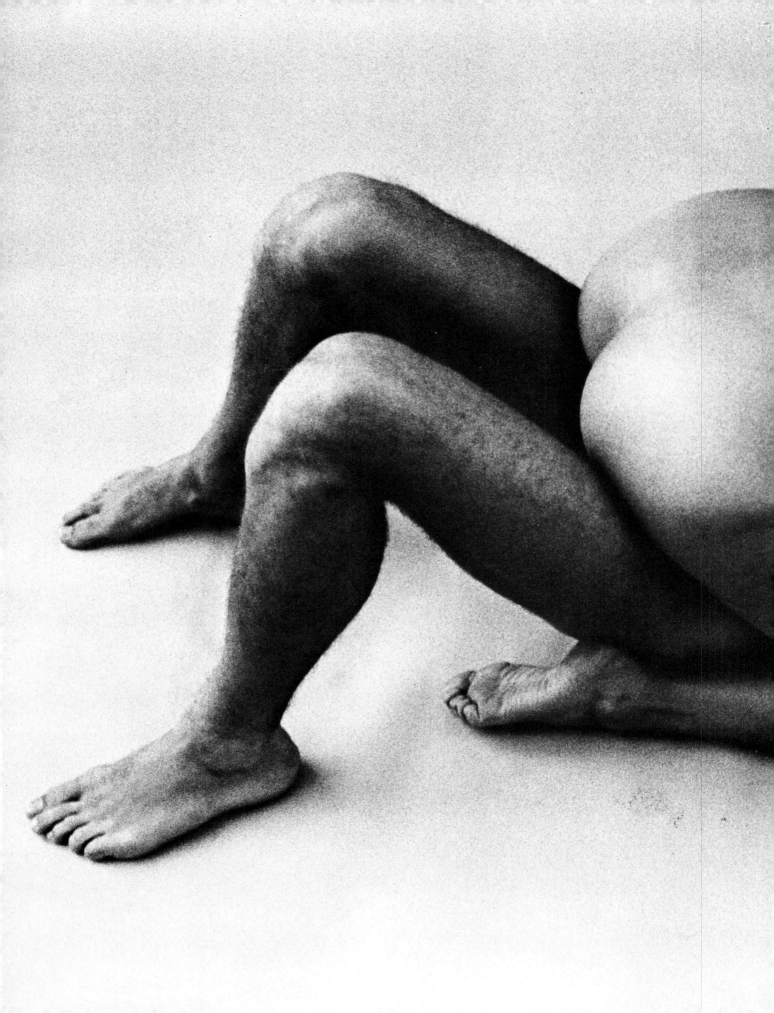

uterus A hollow muscular organ inside the female body, situated at the upper end of the **vagina,** between the bladder and the rectum. (See also **genitals.**)

The upper part of the uterus is connected with the **Fallopian tubes,** through which the **ovum** enters after **ovulation.** The neck of the uterus, which is called **cervix,** opens towards the vagina, from which the **spermatozoa** enter after **ejaculation** from the **penis** during **coitus.** In the case of a **conception,** the fertilized ovum develops into an **embryo** and then into a **fetus** inside the uterus until, at the end of the **pregnancy,** it is expelled through the vagina during **birth.**

vagina
The female sex organ. Part of the internal female **genitals.**

The vagina is a muscular tube which extends from the **vulva** to the **uterus.** The external opening of the vagina, which is below that of the **urethra,** is covered by the inner lips (labia minora) and, in a virgin, it may be partly closed by the **hymen.**

The vagina serves three main functions: the release of the menstrual flow, the reception of the **penis** during **coitus,** and the delivery of the baby during **birth.**

The walls of the vagina are lubricated by secretions which are slightly acid and which serve as a protection against certain infections. (Vaginal douches are unnecessary and may be harmful.) The vagina belongs to the **erogenous zones.** The vaginal secretions increase during sexual **excitement,** thus facilitating the insertion of the penis for the purpose of coitus. During coitus, the walls of the vagina, which are very elastic, keep close contact with the penis, and the coital friction eventually leads to **orgasm** and to the **ejaculation** of **sperm,** which subsequently moves from the vagina into the uterus. A woman can also learn to control her vaginal muscles.

For the delivery of a child, the vagina expands considerably. After the birth, it shrinks back to its normal size.

vaginism
Vaginal spasms. Painful contraction of the **vagina** and adjacent areas of the body.

Vaginism can occur as a result of sexual fear and apprehension or because previous intercourse was painful. The vaginal cramp, which begins as soon as the vagina is touched, prevents the insertion of the **penis** and thus makes **coitus** impossible.

Occasionally one can encounter rumors that such vaginal cramps occurred not before, but during coitus, thus trapping the penis and requiring the help of a physician for the separation of sexual partners. Such rumors are usually based on fantasies and exaggerations, although vaginal cramps after insemination can be observed in certain animals, such as cats and dogs.

Women who suffer from vaginism can be helped by professional treatment.

vanity

Vanity motivates people to emphasize and develop certain traits that seem to make them more popular. A certain amount of vanity is natural and healthy, as no one can live without self-acceptance and self-respect.

The first traces of vanity in a young person are symptoms of his growing sense of identity, and of his awareness that he may be attractive to a potential sexual partner.

Vanity can, of course, easily be carried to the extreme of self-adulation and disregard for others. However, the same disregard can result from a total lack of vanity, as in the case of persons who completely neglect their appearance and become unpleasant and sloppy. In both instances the cause is emotional insecurity.

variety

Variety in sexual matters is helpful as well as risky. Helpful, because it can increase pleasure; risky, because it can strain and even ruin a sexual relationship.

However, the excitement of the new does not necessarily have to be gained at the expense of emotional security. For example, steady sexual partners can pleasantly surprise each other by varying their attitudes and approaches, by renewing their courtship, by wearing different clothes, or by trying different coital **positions.** Such helpful variety is possible as long as both partners continue to study each other's preferences, and try to fulfill each other's secret desires. A monotonous repetition of the same sexual behavior patterns betrays a lack of sensitivity and imagination. As a result, the relationship becomes predictable and boring. On the other hand, sexual variety sought by a frequent change of partners is equally likely to lead to dissatisfaction, because the emotional contact remains superficial. The will to respond to a sexual partner's need for variety is a sign of true love. It can substantially strengthen a sexual relationship.

vasectomy

Male **sterilization** operation.

The operation consists of the closing of a small tube on each side of the **scrotum**—the "vas deferens"—which carries the sperm. This closing of the spermatic ducts makes a man infertile, although by no means impotent. The result should be considered final. Continuing research is improving the surgical techniques for a reversal of the operation, but its success cannot be guaranteed.

Vasectomy is a minor operation, and is usually performed in the doctor's office under local anesthesia. Voluntary sterilization is 100% effective as a method of **birth control,** and is legal in all 50 states.

venereal diseases

(Literally: diseases attributed to Venus) A euphemism for a number of contagious diseases which are communicated mainly by **sexual intercourse.** The most dangerous and most common of these diseases are **gonorrhea** and **syphilis.**

There are, of course, many other diseases that can be communicated by intimate physical contact, such as the common cold, tuberculosis, and all other infectious diseases. However, the diseases commonly known as venereal diseases can be singled out as a distinct group because they are almost exclusively transmitted by close skin contact with an infected sexual partner, and they usually first affect the sexual organs by which this contact has been made.

Whether someone has been infected with a venereal disease can be determined only by a professional medical diagnosis. In many states of the U.S. a doctor is authorized to test and treat a **minor** for a venereal disease without the consent of parents. However, in the case of a suspected infection, shame and embarrassment should not be allowed to prevent anyone, no matter how young, from seeking immediate medical help. Neither does the lack of money have to be an obstacle, as free treatment can be obtained from public health services.

In their early stages, both gonorrhea and syphilis can be cured quickly and easily. However, without proper treatment, gonorrhea can lead to sterility, and syphilis can lead to severe disability and death.

The only reliable protection against catching a venereal disease is the avoidance of sexual intercourse with infected partners. Washing or douching after sexual intercourse or the use of a **condom** by males offers only partial protection.

virgin

A sexually mature girl who has not had any **sexual intercourse.**

virginity

The physical and psychological state of a girl or woman before her **defloration.** The term is sometimes also applied to males before their **first sexual intercourse.**

Occasionally, the word "virginity" is also used as a synonym for **chastity** or sexual **abstinence.** As such, it is considered by some as a virtue and an ideal worth pursuing for its own sake. This philosophy is usually also connected with some sort of private or institutional **asceticism.** (See also **celibacy.**) Some women, who hope for a life-long exclusive love relationship with only one man, decide to preserve their virginity for their future husband.

In the past, a woman's intact **hymen** was often considered proof of her virginity. However, such supposed evidence is unrealiable, since the hymen may have been broken by causes other than **coitus.** In some cases, the hymen may even be absent. On the other hand, it is very well possible for a woman to engage in many forms of **sexual intercourse** without rupturing her hymen. (See also **petting.**)

199

Among our ancestors, female virginity was often associated with all sorts of magical and mystical beliefs, and it has always been valued much more highly than the virginity of males. (See **double standard.**) This higher regard for female virginity is also reflected in numerous religious beliefs, folk tales, and popular superstitions. In many fairy tales, for example, certain tasks can be accomplished only by a virgin.

The obsession with female virginity has its roots in the fact that, in the patriarchal societies of the past, women were the property of men. (See **father, patriarchy.**) Even today there are many men who believe sexual intercourse with a virgin to be particularly pleasurable. This belief may be related to certain feelings of sexual inadequacy (she will not be able to make unfavorable comparisons) or to certain sadistic impulses (she may experience pain during defloration). Certain other men prefer a virgin because they trust them to be free from **venereal diseases.** However, fears of infection can be much more reliably alleviated by means of a medical test.

virility

(From Latin "vir": man) A term sometimes used instead of either **masculinity** or male sexual **potency.**

voyeur

A person who enjoys watching people taking their clothes off, masturbating, or having sexual intercourse.

People who, for their own sexual arousal and satisfaction, totally depend on such watching of others suffer from voyeurism, which is a sexual **perversion.**

vulva

Female genital orifice or, more precisely, the external female **genitals** consisting of the outer lips (labia majora), the inner lips (labia minora), the **clitoris** and the opening of the urethra (the tract through which the urine is released).

The vulva opens during **sexual excitement.** (See also **first sexual intercourse.**)

wedding
The **marriage** ceremony.

wedding night
Traditionally, the first night after the wedding was considered the appropriate time for a woman's **defloration** and **first sexual intercourse.**

The wedding night thus became a crucial (and often excruciating) experience for a married couple. Ideally, the wife was a **virgin** without any sexual feelings or even theoretical knowledge of sexual matters. She was expected to submit passively to the desires of her husband, who now had to "prove his masculinity" by arousing and satisfying her. The first "successful" **coitus** was considered the "consummation of marriage." Under these circumstances, the wedding night was often more of an ordeal than a pleasure.
Today the night after the wedding no longer has this exaggerated importance. Modern couples are usually well informed and, in many cases, they have had **sexual intercourse** in one form or another before the wedding. They did not marry in order to have sex, but because they love each other and want to spend the rest of their lives together.

wet dream
A slang expression referring to the fact that occasionally men may involuntarily experience **orgasm** and an **ejaculation** of semen in their sleep. (See also **sexual dream.**)

whore
A female **prostitute.**

wife
The female partner in a **marriage.**

withdrawal method
See **coitus interruptus.**

woman   An adult human **female.**

The most decisive biological difference between the sexes is the fact that women alone are able to conceive (see **conception, pregnancy**) and give **birth** to children. This biological difference has, in the past, been used to define women as destined for motherhood, at the exclusion of nearly every other aspect of the female human potential. However, the beginning **emancipation** of women has also begun to redefine their traditional roles and, consequently, change the relationship between the sexes. As soon as a woman can decide by herself—even against the will of her husband—if and when she wants to accept the responsibilities of motherhood, the traditional concept of fatherhood cannot remain unaffected. (See **birth control, father, mother.**) The decision to have children concerns both parents and demands a commitment from both the man and the woman. As a consequence of this newly shared responsibility it has become more obvious than ever that procreation and **sexuality** are two different things. The growing realization of this truth, and the increasing influence of women in all spheres of life, must ultimately lead to new forms of human interrelations. (See **equality of the sexes.**) Although the emancipation of women is still far from complete, it has already become apparent that the traditional distinctions between male and female spheres of life are obsolete. The world of today, still largely dominated by traditional male values, must tomorrow become a place which is shaped and interpreted through a combined effort of both sexes. (See **patriarchy.**)

women's liberation   A radical social movement devoted to the **emancipation** of women.

zoophilia Sexual intercourse with animals. (See **perversion.**)

zygote A cell resulting from the union of two reproductive cells. In human reproduction: an egg that has been fertilized by a sperm cell. (See **conception, ovum, spermatozoa.**)

Glossary of Sexual Slang

One of the main problems of sex education is the lack of simple, accurate, and acceptable words in which to talk about sex. This is more than an inconvenience, as was recognized by the Federal Commission on Obscenity and Pornography, which states in its official report:

"The Commission believes that much of the "problem" regarding materials which depict explicit sexual activity stems from the inability or reluctance of people in our society to be open and direct in dealing with sexual matters. This most often manifests itself in the inhibition of talking openly and directly about sex. Professionals use highly technical language when they discuss sex; others of us escape by using euphemisms—or by not talking about sex at all. Direct and open conversation about sex between parent and child is too rare in our society."

This lack of communication is not easily overcome. Both abstract scientific terms and pious euphemisms seem strangely awkward and inappropriate for what is, after all, a natural part of everybody's life. Unfortunately, the only existing alternative, the so-called "four-letter words," usually create even greater uneasiness and embarrassment. Although they are often graphic, and sometimes ironic, indeed even humorous, they are generally felt to be "obscene," "filthy," or "dirty," and therefore cannot be used in public or in polite private conversation. Nevertheless, in the absence of legitimate sex education, these slang expressions are often the only sexual terms a young person knows, and since they never appear in the average educational book, he may find himself deprived of any further instruction.

It is for this reason that the authors of the present encyclopedia have felt obliged to provide a glossary of sexual slang. It will enable even those young people who are unfamiliar with the professional terminology to find the correct information.

SLANG	MEANING	SEE UNDER
AC/DC	ambisexual	**ambisexual**
ass	buttocks or rectum	**anal intercourse**
to ball	to have sexual intercourse	**sexual intercourse**
balls	testicles	**testicles**
to beat off	to masturbate	**masturbation**
to beat one's meat	to masturbate	**masturbation**
to blow somebody	to fellate somebody	**fellatio**
blow job	fellatio	**fellatio**
bull dyke	a masculine looking lesbian	**homosexuality**
butch	masculine looking	**masculinity**
cherry	hymen	**hymen**
clap	gonorrhea	**gonorrhea**
closet queen	a male homosexual who does not admit his homosexuality	**homosexuality**
cock	penis	**penis**
cocksucker	a male homosexual	**homosexuality**
to come	to have an orgasm	**orgasm**
to cornhole	to have anal intercourse	**anal intercourse**
cunt	vagina	**vagina**
dick	penis	**penis**
to do somebody	to fellate somebody	**fellatio**
drag	clothing of the opposite sex	**transvestite**
drag queen	a male homosexual who sometimes wears female clothes	**homosexuality**
dyke	a female homosexual	**homosexuality**
to eat somebody	to have oral intercourse	**oral intercourse**
to eat somebody out	to engage in cunnilingus	**cunnilingus**
to eat pussy	to engage in cunnilingus	**cunnilingus**
fag, faggot	a male homosexual	**homosexuality**
fairy	a male homosexual	**homosexuality**
fruit	a male homosexual	**homosexuality**
to fuck	to have sexual intercourse	**coitus**
to go down on somebody	to fellate somebody	**fellatio**
hard-on	erection	**erection**
horny	sexually excited	**excitement**
to jack off	to masturbate	**masturbation**
to jerk off	to masturbate	**masturbation**
to knock up	to make pregnant	**pregnancy**
lez	a female homosexual (lesbian)	**homosexuality**
to make somebody	to have sexual intercourse	**sexual intercourse**
nuts	testicles	**testicles**
prick	penis	**penis**

SLANG	MEANING	SEE UNDER
pussy	vagina	**vagina**
queen	a male homosexual	**homosexuality**
queer	homosexual	**homosexuality**
to rim somebody	to lick somebody's rectal opening	**anilingus**
to rub off	to masturbate (females)	**masturbation**
to screw	to have sexual intercourse	**coitus**
s/m	sadistic/masochistic	**perversion**
to suck somebody	to fellate somebody	**fellatio**
swishy	effeminate	**masculinity**
tits	breasts	**breasts**
trade	an ambisexual male	**ambisexual**
VD	venereal disease	**venereal diseases**
to whack off	to masturbate	**masturbation**